Save Your Career

Save Your Career

Thriving in an AI World

Stan Schatt

BEP
BUSINESS EXPERT PRESS
Leader in applied, concise business books

Save Your Career: Thriving in an AI World

Cover design by Cassandra Kronstedt

Interior design by S4Carlisle Publishing Services, Chennai, India

First published in 2026 by
Business Expert Press, LLC
222 East 46th Street, New York, NY 10017
www.businessexpertpress.com

ISBN-13: 978-1-60649-843-9 (paperback)
ISBN-13: 978-1-60649-851-4 (e-book)

Business Career Development Collection

First edition: 2026

10 9 8 7 6 5 4 3 2 1

EU SAFETY REPRESENTATIVE
Mare Nostrum Group B.V.
Doelen 72
4831 GR Breda
The Netherlands
gpsr@mare-nostrum.co.uk

This book is dedicated to Jane, my wife and best friend

Contents

Contents

List of Figures

Description

Do you fight AI, run from it, or make it your ultimate competitive advantage?

The workplace is shifting rapidly, but you don't have to be left behind. The secret isn't escaping technology—it's making a calculated, fact-based decision about your next move. Whether your goal is to supercharge your current role or make a strategic pivot into a safer industry, this book delivers a step-by-step blueprint to future-proof your livelihood.

Inside, you will discover how to:

- **Identify Safe Havens:** Pinpoint which industries are most resilient to automation and where new opportunities are booming.
- **Optimize Your Job Hunt:** Use advanced tech tools to bypass automated resume filters, uncover hidden job openings, and build an irresistible LinkedIn presence.
- **Ace the Interview:** Leverage cutting-edge prep strategies to stand out in a competitive market and fast-track your networking reach.
- **Become an In-House Leader:** Validate your skills quickly so you can guide your current company through its own digital transformation.

Save Your Career is the definitive guide for professionals ready to stop worrying about the future and start engineering it. Packed with concrete, actionable advice, this book helps you analyze your existing skills and map out the perfect career path for tomorrow's economy.

Preface

Twelve Different Careers

Talk about career changers. My wife tells people that she's been married to 12 different men. On my birthday she gave me a scrapbook chronicling my professional journey including 30 different business cards. My mother always told me that I would be a doctor. I understand now why she pushed me in that direction since she lived through the Depression and felt that doctors were always paid, regardless of economic conditions. In fact, at one time, becoming a doctor was the golden ticket to financial success. I moved eagerly into that career track starting with an undergraduate pre-med chemistry emphasis. I even took a job as an autopsy assistant. No experience goes to waste because I used some of those experiences when I wrote a mystery that was set in a hospital.

I realized when I attended medical school at the University of Colorado that I wouldn't be happy with that career and that it was my mother's dream and not mine. I met a student in his senior year there who told me I should listen to my heart because he had decided medicine wasn't for him, but he already was in too deep with student loans to change his career direction. I sometimes wonder whether he wound up embracing medicine eventually or feel chained to it because of his financial debit.

I discuss a number of aptitude tests in Chapter 4 that you can take to help you determine your strengths and interests as well as tools to match them with careers and job titles that match them. In my case, I had taken some aptitude tests and was told I could be anything in the world except an engineer. Why? Apparently, I scored abysmally low when it came to a test that determined my ability to deal with spatial relationships. In that test I had to look at objects and imagine what they would look like turned upside down and sideways or backward. I never saw the connection with medicine, but I realized later that spatial relationships are very important for a surgeon. After all, a doctor needs to know what lies behind and around an organ while operating. So, as I joke with my wife, many people are alive today because I chose not to become a doctor. I help you do some soul searching in Chapter 2 to determine whether or not you really want a new career or simply want to find another job doing what you do or did previously or a similar job, perhaps with an enhancement to make it attractive in an artificial intelligence (AI) world.

I had always loved literature and had thought at times of becoming a professor, so I made the transition to graduate school and earned a PhD. I became a university professor and taught at several schools including the University of Southern California, the University of Houston, and even Tokyo University on a Fulbright. I published regularly and received citations for outstanding teaching, so it seemed like I was set on a career path that would carry me along through 40 years of teaching before I would be let out to pasture as an Emeritus Professor.

Life has a way of surprising you. Because I had a background that included a science major, I was the only professor in my department who agreed to serve as thesis adviser for a graduate student working on his master's degree. Since he was in the process of changing his own career from professional mainframe programmer to literature professor, he wanted to do a study that utilized computers, something very new at the time. I was fascinated by the direction I thought the computer industry would take and decided I really wanted to be part of that industry. My wife agreed to cover our expenses by taking a teaching job, and I went to school for a year to update my credentials with an MBA that included some computer training.

The difficulty in changing careers is compounded by the need to convince decision makers that you are really qualified for this new career. That's why Chapter 6 covers networking and social media. The more people you talk with, the more chance of a connection with a decision maker. I had found an administrative job running the City of Phoenix Police Department Equal Opportunity Employment program. I worked closely with police personnel, and my office was right near that of a crusty old veteran who administered the polygraph to police officers accused of wrongdoing. Once again, no experience is wasted because I later used that experience in a police procedure novel I wrote. As far as networking goes, while working in the police department I happened to talk with an older woman who worked as a secretary. I mentioned my interest in computers, and she told me her husband was in charge of all computer training at Honeywell's Process Control Division (Think mainframe computers). I told her I'd love to meet him, and she arranged for me to meet him for lunch.

So, I had to keep my career goal in mind. I had about 45 minutes minus actual chewing time during the lunch to convince someone I had never met that he should hire me. That's where transferable skills come into play. After all, what is technical training of customers but teaching? Over lunch I convinced the manager that I could learn the material if he put me through the training program and then I could train Honeywell's customers in assembly language programming. Actually, it was a daunting task since the training consisted of four weeks of full-day training and many of the customers used these computers where they worked—nuclear power plants.

I did the training job, and fortunately none of my students set off any nuclear explosions where they worked. Still, my wife and I longed to get back to California. When a business manager job opened up at the University of California San Diego's campus, I applied and was hired. That worked out great until the university had to cut personnel because a bill cutting property tax had a negative impact on University of California budgets. Like so many of you reading this book, I was laid off. At that time personal computers were becoming available, and I could visualize just how popular they would become. So, I went through a period of working in the personal computer industry. That included a job managing a retail computer store (remember when they existed?) and a job selling computers as an account executive for AT&T.

During this time in the computer field, I became thoroughly immersed in the technology. I lived and breathed it. One day I saw an opening to teach computer technology at a trade college. I did that job for a number of years while I read the trade journals. I noticed that stories often included quotes from people known as "industry analysts." Who were those people? I did some research and discovered their jobs were to become experts in certain industries and technologies and to speak on the subject and also write articles that clients would pay to read. So, let's look at those transferable skills: Speaking before groups sounds a lot like training or teaching. Writing articles sounds a lot like the articles I wrote as a professor. Becoming an expert on a subject sounded a lot like what professors were expected to do. In other words, all the major skills were transferable from my previous jobs. That job led to others in a career that spanned two decades. It was a career that AI would be hard-pressed to do, and one that I loved. I even wrote a book[1] describing how to use transferable skills to make a lateral career change salarywise rather than starting at the bottom level along with people just out of school. In the case of this book, the emphasis was on how to move to a green-oriented career. In Chapter 3, I discuss how one option is to take an existing career and add an AI element.

Identifying the key decision maker is crucial, particularly when changing careers because you need to convince that person that your transferable skills make you an ideal candidate. I found a local company that hired industry analysts and found out that its Research Director would be representing his company at a huge convention in Las Vegas. I took a day off from my job at the time, paid my own way for the day trip, and arrived early in the morning. I finally located the man I sought. The result was an interview once he returned from Las Vegas. I did my due diligence researching the company and the industry until I felt I already worked there. I received a job offer soon after the interview due in no small part to the research I'd done. The key point I would make about this particular incident is that the company had not advertised a position. It created the position once I had the interview. That shows the importance of researching a company and an industry. Instead of looking at 700+ resumes, the decision maker only looked at mine.

My point in recounting my personal experiences is that I understand the anguish of considering a major career change as well as the difficult road from that decision to an actual job in a new career. I understand the need to credential oneself to fill in gaps that remain in your educational background. Chapter 5 covers the easiest road to establishing your credibility for a new career through certificate programs which tend to require a few months rather than years. If credential programs had been available several years ago, I would have taken that route instead of taking an entire year to pick up the information I needed for the new career.

Because AI plays such a major role in hiring today, I have included a chapter on how to use AI tools to improve your cover letters and resumes as well as a chapter on using AI to help you prepare for your interviews as well as outfox AI software designed to rate applicants. Because social networking is so critical today in your career change, I have included a chapter on that subject as well.

Finally, I wrote a book a couple of years ago on the impact of AI and other technologies on jobs.[2] I spent a great deal of time researching the impact of AI on various careers, and I've included that information in Chapter 1. It would be silly to go through all the effort to change careers and then jump into one that soon will be swallowed up by AI. So, I point to a number of limitations of AI that make certain careers much more likely to survive AI as well as robots that use AI.

Because everyone needs encouragement when pursuing a career change, I have included a section in each chapter called "Spotlight on a Career Changer." The ages of these career changers vary considerably as do their previous jobs and careers.

I congratulate you on your brave decision to consider a career change, whether you are in your 30s or in your 50s; it takes courage because of the temporary but significant impact on yourself as well as on your family. For those of you who are 50+ I cover careers where age is not as much a factor in hiring because they chose careers and industries that are growing rapidly and need people desperately. One point I would like to make is that from this point forward changing careers is likely to become a normal way of life. Employees are likely to have to be flexible enough to reinvent themselves several times during a lifetime in order to stay ahead of the inroads AI makes on various industries. Hopefully this book will provide you with a framework to use every time you decide to explore yet another new career.

My personal saga includes a number of different careers. People in the future are going to have to be agile enough to change careers several times as AI starts to make inroads. The key is to use your transferable skills and to acquire the information you need through certificate programs online. It is critical to do the research you need to identify careers and jobs as well as companies that are a good fit for you.

CHAPTER 1

The Impact of AI on the Job Market

More and More Companies Are Laying off People

Companies are laying off people at an alarming rate. In 2025, more than 1.1 million Americans were laid off from their jobs.[1] It's not your imagination. Artificial intelligence (AI) is breathing down the necks of anyone who works in an office environment. When IBM announced it was laying off 8,000 people over the next few years, it specified that the layoffs would take place in areas such as Human Relations, Accounting, finance, and other "noncustomer-facing roles."[2] Microsoft did a study of the jobs most likely to be lost to AI, and its list went well beyond accounting and finance. It concluded that the jobs least at risk are blue-collar positions that require hands-on operations. Microsoft included such positions as orderly, dredge operator, logging equipment operators, and foundry mold and coremakers.[3] What about the jobs most at risk? The list included those jobs focusing on writing, speaking/sales, teaching, and analysis.

Historians were number one on the list of jobs and careers in jeopardy. Post-secondary business teachers and economics teachers as well as teachers of farm and home management made the list as well. What about writers? Authors, editors, journalists, proofreaders, public relations personnel, and technical writers are on the list. For those who speak for a living, jobs and careers in danger include translators, services salespeople, and customer service personnel. Likely it will be a robot with AI that assumes some of these roles. Clerks and analysts as well as mathematicians are on the danger list as well.[4] Nexford University's crystal ball points to the rapid demise of customer service reps, receptionists, accountants, bookkeepers, salespeople, researchers, analysts, insurance underwriters, retail, and warehouse workers.[5]

Cognizant recently published a study that confirmed Microsoft's findings. It listed the positions likely to be impacted by AI based on the percentage of tasks associated by the jobs that could be done now by AI[6]:

1. Financial managers: 84 percent impacted
2. Computer and mathematical roles: 67 percent impacted
3. Business and financial operations: 60 percent to 68 percent impacted
4. Office and administration support: 60 percent to 68 percent impacted
5. Legal occupations: 63 percent impacted
6. Management jobs, including C-suite: 60 percent impacted

Imagine you work in an insurance office. That paper-heavy environment is a perfect target for AI. Does a customer need help in selecting which insurance policy is right? AI can go through a decision tree to arrive at the right choice very easily. It is becoming clear why this next technology job bloodbath will be so much worse than previous ones. The arrival of personal computers in the 1980s destroyed the secretary position which later was replaced with administrative assistants. Today anyone whose position involves working with paper or data is in great danger today from AI.

Remember when a well-meaning friend of his parents whispered the field "plastics" to Dustin Hoffman in the movie, The Graduate? Someone who went into that field in the 1960s would have done very well indeed. The best college students were promised success a few years ago if they went into computer programming. Unfortunately, AI is moving incredibly quickly to subsume many of these jobs. Now it can write code. In fact, one executive said he no longer hired beginning programmers but hired senior programmers to solve problems. If you're a recent college graduate in computer software, you likely are having more trouble than you ever expected landing an entry-level position.

When I was younger, the "golden ticket" to success was an MD. Doctors in the 1960s joined country clubs and lived in the best neighborhoods. Recently, the "golden ticket" to success that parents drilled into their children included not just the benefits of careers in computer software but also the safety of working for really large companies. Amazon is the poster child to demonstrate the lack of safety, even in administrative positions, at a very large company. It recently announced two major layoffs that totaled 35,000 employees or 9 percent of its total workforce. The reason given for the layoffs was that AI would improve the company's efficiency. CEO Andrew Jassy was quoted as saying,"

> "As we roll out more Generative AI and agents, it should change the way our work is done. We will need fewer people doing some of the jobs that are being done today, and more people doing other types of jobs."[7]

By the end of February 2026 several major companies announced layoffs because AI was making them more efficient. The industries affected included Retail (Target 500 employees), Financial Services (Mastercard 1,400 employees and Citibank's plans for cuts up to 20,000 employees), and technology (Meta Platforms around 1,400 employees as part of a "strategic shift to AI").[8] Remember Jack Dorsey, the founder of Twitter? He now runs Block, a company that owns Square, Cash App, and Tidal. The company is in the payments business. Dorsey announced on February 26, 2026, that his company was laying off 40 percent of its workforce or 4,000 employees because AI tools enable the company to run more efficiently with fewer people.[9]

The News Is Getting Worse, Not Better

JP Morgan's researchers have been studying the job market. They've noted how AI has impacted recent college graduates in the areas of computer engineering, graphic design, industrial engineering, and architecture. One scary takeaway from this study is that the researchers noted that employment across several key segments had "plateaued." A second observation the JP Morgan research study noted was that the jobs of "knowledge workers" are threatened by AI and pointed to the danger to those employees in "cognitive" fields such as scientists. So, it is not just the college graduate applying for a first job who now is grappling with the impact of AI, but also the seasoned highly degreed employees.[10] Major consulting firms studied the possible impact of AI on jobs and came to radically different conclusions. McKinsey's analysts predicted that nearly 70 million American workers would have to find new occupations by 2030 because of AI[11] while Bain and Company's analysts concluded that 20 percent to 25 percent of workers would be impacted.[12]

The frightening news for workers is that while a majority of the Fortune 500 have begun to deploy AI, these companies have not yet fully integrated AI with their operations. As they begin to do so, the loss of jobs will likely accelerate. Right now, companies are laying off people based on AI's potential, not its actual performance to date. The CEOs of Ford, Amazon, Salesforce, and JP Morgan Chase have indicated that many of their white-collar jobs will soon disappear.[13]

Many employees lost their jobs in 2025 or early in 2026. Those still employed are often described as "hugging their jobs," meaning they are holding on for dear life, afraid they might be the next to be laid off. So, whether currently employed or currently unemployed, many people are interested in not just changing their jobs, but changing their careers and finding an occupation that has the possibility of growth over the next several years.

Lessons to Be Learned

What lessons can we learn by looking back at previous technology disruptions and their impact on the job market? Around 1900 a reporter for *The London Times* who had visited New York City with its over 10,000 horses in the city forecast that in a decade the entire city would be buried in horse manure.[14] Of course that didn't happen. What did happen was a major technology disruption, in that case it was the automobile. Tens of thousands of people lost their jobs as stable boys, carriage makers, and so on. Some of those people never did change careers and never found work, but most did. Stable boys changed careers and became gas station attendants while carriage makers began assembling automobiles. Later all kinds of new jobs developed centered around the automobile such as marketing director, service repairman, and used car salesman.

When personal computer sales rose as software became available, some people lost their jobs. There was less demand for secretaries or for many positions associated with mainframe computers. Soon, though, all kinds of new types of jobs were created including software engineering, computer repair, and computer security. The key to understanding this cycle, though, is that the disruption caused by the introduction of AI could be fundamentally different. One reason is that rather than simply being a dumb machine that marginally improved efficiency, AI is smart and becoming smarter every day. Tasks it cannot perform today it might be able to perform tomorrow.

Spotlight on a Career Changer

From University Administrator to Social Care Worker

COVID-19 had an impact on a number of jobs and that includes Fiona Jack's career as a university administrator. She searched for meaningful work and discovered a part-time position as an animal care assistant in a cat rescue organization. She was elated when she interviewed and was hired. She found the work satisfying, but realized she needed something that paid more. Fiona found a local charity that offered an eight-week paid training course. She took it and then started working as a caregiver. She's found the work physically and mentally demanding but satisfying and is able to pick up extra shifts if she needs more money.[15]

While it is true that some related jobs will be created (think repairman for robots with AI as an example), AI agents and applications will subsume many more jobs that they create, at least for the foreseeable future. Dario Amodei, one of the founders of Anthropic, a leading AI company, warned on *60 Minutes* that AI could wipe out half of all entry-level white-collar jobs and spike unemployment to 10 percent to 20 percent in the next one to five years. He pointed specifically to entry-level consultants, lawyers, financial professionals, and many "white-collar service industries."[16]

A Strategy for Success

So, what is a person currently laid off or hugging a job he or she hates supposed to do? Hopefully they will find the answer in this book. The strategy I will suggest is a combination of either becoming part of the workforce that will need to work with AI in the near future or follow the baseball advice of Wee Willy Keeler who in the early 1900s advised batters to "hit the ball where they ain't." In other words, find your way to a career niche that is well beyond AI's capabilities for a number of years.

That's not to say that taking Keeler's advice is a permanent solution. It is likely that people will have to be agile enough to retrain a number of times during their working lives in order to stay employable. I'll discuss how to make that possible later in this book. So, let's begin by understanding the sheer number of people in the same boat; they want to change careers but are too fearful to act or they want to act but don't know where to start.

The Number of People Wanting to Change Careers Is Growing

In 2024, approximately 59 percent of U.S. professionals were focused on finding a new job, indicating a high level of career mobility.[17] *The Wall Street Journal* reported that the number of people wanting to change careers reached a 10-year high.[18] Imagine more than half of the U.S. workforce actively focused on finding new jobs. Some of the statistics on career changers is fascinating. Over 70 percent of Gen Z and millennial workers are considering changing jobs or careers followed by 51 percent of Gen X and 33 percent of baby boomers. The average age of a career changer is 39, while the average person will change jobs 12 times in a career.[19] So, if you are employed but thinking about a new job or career change or unemployed and seriously looking at a career change, you are not alone.

I'm going to describe a systematic approach to career changing that assures you find the right career for yourself and one that is not likely to be decimated by AI. Given the number of unhappy workers, it is no wonder job seekers report sending out hundreds of resumes without any responses. Don't worry, though. Later in this book I'll offer several techniques you can use to improve your response rate and get interviews. I'll go one step further then and discuss how to ace the interview. Crazy behavior is doing the same thing over and over when it doesn't work. You'll learn how to approach the job hunt very differently and even learn how to use AI tools to outwit the AI screening a company's applications.

So, congratulations on taking the first enormous step toward your next career. You've recognized the problem AI poses for the entire workplace and you've decided to take action. In the next several chapters you'll learn a lot about yourself as well as learn a lot about how to get a step up on other job seekers.

Conclusion

Fortune 500 companies are laying off people at astonishing rates leaving those who survive the first wave of dismissals "hugging" their jobs and afraid to let go. Companies are banking on AI improving their efficiency. As AI's capabilities improve, white-collar workers who deal primarily with paper and information are at risk. The key is to be agile and find niches where it is not economic to utilize AI. The number of people seeking to change their careers is growing each year. This book offers a systematic approach to career changing.

CHAPTER 2

The First Steps Toward a Career Change

A New Job or a New Career?

At this point you might be unemployed or still holding onto a job that you do not love. I would ask the same question regardless of your current status: Do you want a new job in the same field, or are you ready to change careers? It's not an easy question to answer. You need to do some soul searching to discover what you like and dislike about the job. Is it simply a boss you couldn't stand? Is it a problem limited to that particular company? Do you feel burned-out? Perhaps you feel unappreciated. Perhaps the pay is low or the chances of advancement are very limited. Do you enjoy the type of work you do? Imagine, if you can, doing the same work in a different work environment. Would that be satisfying? One analyst suggests you look at the skills and experience required for the next level up on your current career ladder. If your job is not giving you the knowledge and experience needed for the next level up, the likelihood is that you never will gain that promotion doing what you do.[1]

Reasons for Dissatisfaction

Another source of job dissatisfaction is if you work in a toxic work environment. I remember one place I worked at installed a new CEO who had never been a CEO. His style was to belittle anyone who asked a question he didn't like or didn't go along with whatever he said. At one companywide meeting an employee asked an innocent question about bonuses and was told in no uncertain terms that not only was he not getting one, but that he was skirting on thin ice when it came to his job. Another person at a company where I worked soon realized that the CEO had once, a long time ago, held a job title similar to his. The CEO constantly second-guessed him and made it clear that whatever he did, it would not be good enough when compared to what the CEO had done years earlier.

Advantages of a New Job Instead of a New Career

The reason these questions are so important is that there are a lot of issues associated with changing careers that are not necessarily associated with simply finding a new job in the same industry. For one thing, you already have a network of colleagues and perhaps even customers who know you and who can help you reach out to the right people within other companies. You might even know ex-colleagues who now work at a competitor who can put in a good word for you. Second, you likely do not need to credential yourself to qualify for a position as you would likely need to do to change careers.

Finally, the time between jobs is probably going to be shorter if you are just looking for a new job in the same field since you will not have to factor in the time credentialing yourself or the time convincing employers that your transferable skills are ideal for a career change. Also, it is easier for people who have worked with you or even for you to write recommendations for the same type of job with a different company. Finally, since the interval between jobs is likely to be shorter if you're just looking for a job in the same occupation, the economic pressure will be less burdensome.

Still, you don't want to be jumping from the frying pan into the fire. Chapter 1 pointed out the enormous pressure that AI is putting on specific industries that want to justify their financial investment in that technology. If you were laid off as a result of your company's efforts to be "more efficient" by turning to AI, there is a likelihood that the next company in the same industry will soon be looking at deploying AI and planning layoffs. So, if you are planning to find another job in the same industry, be sure to read Chapter 5 to find out if the industry is relatively safe for the time being from AI-inspired job cuts.

Yet another possibility is that you would like to stay in the same industry despite the looming presence of AI adoption. Chapter 3 will help you consider how you can combine your current skills and job experience with some AI credentialing to make yourself valuable to companies deploying AI.

Taking Your Finances into Account

If you are still hugging the job that you hate and contemplating a career shift, it is a good time to begin saving your money in a rainy-day account to be used to help support yourself between jobs. You need to do a complete check of your finances, including your retirement accounts. If it becomes necessary, do you have retirement funds to borrow against? Make a list of current expenses and see which ones can be pared down. Do you have three different cable services? Consider choosing the one you watch the most. How often do you treat yourself to a Starbucks in the morning or lunch out? Consider bringing your lunch and coffee from home. You should be able to come up with your minimal monthly expenses that have to be paid. What you will want as a goal is to have several months of money in the bank in reserve. That will prevent a lot of sleepless nights.

While job hunting is a full-time job, you might also consider some of the websites online for part-time remote jobs to help supplement whatever funds you've set aside. Jobs like virtual assistant positions can make it possible to survive until your new job starts. Another necessity is to consider the impact on your family. If you can get your family to buy-into the drastic change in the family's income situation, you'll find it much easier to hunt for another job or even another career.

Finding out More About Yourself

The first step down the path toward a new career is to make the decision you are willing to consider changing careers. Assuming you are open to that possibility, the next step is to find out what kind of jobs and industries match your interests and aptitudes. Chapter 4 will provide you with a list of tests that you can take to learn more about yourself. It is surprising how many people have never taken these kinds of tests. You'll not only learn your interests, but you'll also learn your personal traits, likes and dislikes about the workplace. Imagine being a mid-career professional who has just been laid off. If I ask you how you chose the company that laid you off after 10 years, you might respond that a friend of the family worked there and put in a good word or that you saw an ad and applied. Was it a perfect fit? The answer is probably no, but it was a job and it did pay the bills. Yet, haven't you ever wondered if there was something you really were meant to do, something that utilized so much more of what you have to offer? That's the point of Chapter 4. Depending on the specific test and the fee you pay, you might receive a very detailed 30-page report that analyzes the raw data from your test and offers recommendations. Some of these websites even offer a search capability where you plug in some of the traits your tests revealed and you see a list of occupations and jobs that match well. Who knew you really suited best for an outdoor job in a nonprofit or a remote job where you had more control over your day?

Your Career Center Can Help

If you are a career changer who graduated from a university, be sure to consider contacting the school's career center. I'll use my undergraduate school's career center as an example. It offers an hour-long video conference chat with a career counselor. It also offers a number of assessment tests that can be taken online. It then has an online tool that reveals your assessment with the opportunity to talk with a career counselor about the results. You then can use yet another interactive tool to match your assessment results with what appear to be the best careers and jobs. At this point it is possible to once again talk with a career counselor to learn what certifications are required to make the switch to a new career. The cost? It's free at this particular university, and I'm sure the cost, if there is one, is reasonable at most other universities.

Spotlight on a Career Changer

From Accountant to Freelance Writer

Heidi Borst worked as an accountant until she was 35 when she gave birth to her son. She then spent several years at home taking care of him. At 40 she faced a dilemma because she felt starved for contact with adults and decided returning to the world of finance was not something she wanted to do. A divorce forced her to consider how she could support herself. Because she had an undergraduate degree in journalism, she began writing for a parenting publication. She joined Facebook writing groups and took some online writing classes. To support herself while she transitioned, she took on "content mill" writing, providing nonbylined medical articles for popular health websites. Eventually she found an editor who gave her a chance and the result for her was a national byline followed by several more.[2]

Research, Research, and More Research

Even if you go the university career center route, it's still worthwhile to do some research on your own to ensure you know everything you possibly can about your career switch. Let's say that you've found some industries and careers that match your interests and abilities. The next step is research. You will need to research the leading companies in this new career path, the actual job titles, and the educational and skill sets required. Nothing is ever wasted. You'll use the information you collect on the leading companies in the industries that interest you later when it comes to setting up a social media campaign to meet people from those companies and industries. You'll find that information in Chapter 6. The key question to ask yourself after doing your research is, *What is the fastest way for me to meet these educational requirements?* You'll find a world of credentialing opportunities in Chapter 5. At that point you'll need to do some financial analysis. If you're still employed, it will be a matter of figuring out how long the specific program will take. If you're unemployed, then the question becomes how much money will it take to cover the time you spend credentialing yourself and whether or not it is possible to find some part-time gigs to help cover the costs.

Making a Plan to Credential Yourself

You are going to want to compare and contrast some of the different ways of meeting the educational requirements for the position you've targeted in your new career. It might be a trade-off between time and money.

Some programs might be online and enable you to move as quickly as you're able while others might be part of a community college or university extension program that require weekly attendance. Time is money when you're unemployed, so a lot will go into the decisions you make. We'll address some of those questions in Chapter 5.

Beginning Your Social Media and Networking Campaign

Chapter 6 covers the many ways you can use your existing contacts as well as uncover mentors to help you on your journey. Keep in mind Willie Sutton's famous line about robbing the banks because that's where the money is. You're not going to be robbing any banks, but you will be learning how to associate yourself with people who can help you find your new job in your new career. Once again, this process will require time and research. In fact, think of this entire career changing operation as a research project that will change your life, not one you are doing to satisfy a professor and earn a good grade. This chapter also includes some specific instructions on how to use LinkedIn to your best advantage.

The Job Search

Chapter 7 focuses on your actual job search. You've already identified the career and position you're interested in and credentialed yourself. You've also managed to build a list of people already in the industry who might be able to help you. The advantage you'll have over many job hunters is that you'll utilize the enormous power of AI to fashion cover letters and resumes that will outwit the forces of evil AI that human resources (HR) departments are using to try to screen applications and even throw out those it thinks were created by AI.

The Interview Process

The Interview process is always more difficult for a career changer, but Chapter 8 will provide you with the best ways to address the questions bound to come. You'll learn how you can use AI to give you the world's toughest interview. I remember using many of these techniques when I was preparing for a new job and new career. After substantial practice, I was almost relieved when an interviewer asked me one of the questions I had identified as the very hardest to address. It felt like déjà vu because I had spent so much time practicing my answer. I had this weird sensation that I was watching myself perform flawlessly in a play because my answers just rolled off my tongue naturally and not as if I'd memorized answers. Needless to say, I did get the job, and you also will have a much better shot at success if you follow the detailed advice in Chapter 8.

The next chapter will guide you if you're interested in remaining in the same industry but finding a way to enhance your skills so you can coexist with AI and even become essential to your company's efforts to deploy AI to increase productivity.

Conclusion

The first question you need to ask yourself is whether you simply need a new job in the same industry or whether you need a completely new career. Answering a new career is a more challenging and lengthy process that includes self-discovery to find out your major strengths and interests. It also includes once you've determined a career direction working out the finances to keep you afloat while you begin your job search. You also will need to determine the best way to credential yourself to leverage your transferable skills.

CHAPTER 3

Would You Rather Find an AI-Related Job Path?

Becoming Part of the Solution

After reading about the advances AI is making into various industries, you may come to the conclusion that rather than spend your life dodging and darting around AI inroads, you want to become part of the AI solution. After all, it will be several years before a company could be run completely by AI, and during that time people with the ability to work with AI will be needed. The noose is tightening already, though, a recent report revealed that companies like Google and Meta are already evaluating their employees' performance based on how much they use AI.[1]

Is There a Fit with Your Current Career Skills?

Let's start with three individuals. Mary has a law degree but worries about the inroads AI is making in that field. Bill is an elementary school teacher who worries about AI taking over many of the key parts of teaching that he enjoys. Finally, Frank is a philosophy professor at a university that seems to be cutting back on liberal arts course offerings each year. The number of students majoring in his area have dropped dramatically in the past few years to the point that the school no longer offers a major in philosophy so Frank can only teach basic introductory courses each year.

Mary worries that someday there will be AI judges and AI lawyers. When she does some research, she discovers that experts have identified AI law as an embryonic field that should grow considerably in the future. Mary does not want to go through three more years of law school, but she wonders if there are certificate programs that can provide her with the credentials that she needs to be considered an expert in this new field. The

University of California's Berkeley's Center for Law and Technology offers a wide range of courses. The student needs 11 units for the credential:

- AI Transactions and Licensing (2 units)
- AI in Biotechnology Law (1 unit)
- Advanced IT Contracts: Drafting and Negotiating (1 unit)
- Antitrust and Emerging Technologies (3 units)
- Copyright Law (3 units)
- Corporate Strategy in the Age of AI and Geopolitics (1 unit)
- Cybersecurity Law Fundamentals (1 unit)
- Cybersecurity in Context: Technology, Policy, and Law (2 units)
- Fundamentals of AI Technology (2 units)
- Generative AI in Legal Practice (1 unit)
- Global Regulation of AI (1 unit)
- Hot Topics in AI (Fall) (1 unit)
- Information Privacy Law (3 units)
- Making AI Work for the People (1 unit)
- The Law and Governance of AI (2 units)
- Trust and Safety (1 unit)
- Video Game Law (1 unit)

In addition to UC Berkeley, the University of Southern California offers a "Law and Artificial Intelligence" certificate which focuses on the evolution of AI tools and legal, ethical, and privacy challenges. Coursera offers "AI for Lawyers and Other Advocates," which provides lawyers with knowledge of generative AI. Stanford Law School offers specialized courses on policy and AI in administrative law, while Arizona State University's Law School offers a master of legal studies in AI law degree.

Researchers will tell Mary that she definitely will be able to make use of her law degree in the future, especially if she adds a credential to demonstrate her knowledge of AI. Among the emerging fields are AI Compliance Officer (Ensuring company AI projects meet regulatory standards), Technology Counsel (Focusing on AI licensing and intellectual property matters) and an AI Policy Expert (Working with governments and organizations on AI governance). Onit (onit.com) offers a 90 minutes video class on how lawyers can use generative AI. Coursera (coursera.org) offers a nine-course certificate program titled "AI in Law: Research, Risk, and Legal Drafting Specialization." AI CERTS (aicerts.ai) offers a nine-module certificate program titled AI+ Legal.

Bill loves teaching his sixth-grade class, but he fears there will be AI tutors and he will be relegated to bookkeeping chores. Many of his fellow teachers, like him, are not technology oriented, so the idea of becoming an AI programmer is unrealistic. Still, Bill did some research and discovered there are a number of ways he could demonstrate his willingness to go with the flow and become a real asset to his school and even his school district. Let's start with programs that require on-site attendance at classes. Private schools are usually in the forefront of new trends, but of course they are pricey. The University of San Diego offers a two-semester "Artificial Intelligence in Education" certificate that is pretty comprehensive. Students choose five of the following six classes listed below:

- Introduction to AI and Education
- AI in Student Support and Engagement
- AI for Curriculum Design and Development
- AI in Educational Leadership and Policy
- Navigating Legal and Ethical Boundaries in the AI Classroom

As you can see, for about $1,400 Bill can demonstrate his specific knowledge of AI in the classroom and perhaps become one of his district's leader's in designing curriculum or even leading the deployment of AI. The good news is there are also free programs that don't require on-site attendance. Udemy (Udemy.com) offers a program in AI for Teachers that consists of 5.5 hours of on-demand video that includes a certificate. The courses cover generative AI and even how to use AI music in the classroom. Google and MIT offer courses in generative AI for educators. Alison (alison.com) offers a free course in AI for educators.

In addition, Open AI has launched a certificate program specifically for teachers in grades K-12. Titled "ChatGPT Foundations for Teachers," the program provides teachers with information on how to use AI tools to save time, personalize classroom materials and lesson plans, and apply generative AI to real classroom and administrative tasks. The company also announced that it is developing a free custom version of ChatGPT for educators as part of its partnership with the American Federation of Teachers (https://openai.com/index/openai-certificate-courses/).

Because the government has very strict privacy requirements for using student data, these courses are essential for anyone thinking of adopting AI for a school district. Coursiv (coursiv.io) provides a list of some considerations when deciding on what AI tools to use in a classroom[2]:

- Does the vendor use student data to train its models? (If yes, it fails the FERPA test.)
- Does a signed Data Processing Agreement exist?
- Does the tool hold SOC 2, COPPA, or Common-Sense Privacy certifications?
- How long does the vendor store data, and will they delete it within a defined window (typically 60 days) after contract termination?
- Does the tool meet ADA/Section 508 requirements, especially given DOJ deadlines for school web accessibility in April 2026–2027?
- Has your district IT team approved it?

Just to show you how fast AI is making its way into education, New York City schools as well as school districts in Chicago, Denver, and Charlotte-Mecklenburg (North Carolina) have released AI guides during the past 10 months while some states such as Ohio have statewide rules on the use of AI. One restriction is that AI should not be used to assign grades.[3]

Frank has more options than he realizes. As a philosophy teacher he already is well-versed in the study of ethics. Universities such as Fordham and the University of Illinois at Urbana are offering certificates in the Ethics of AI. Edx (edx.org) offers a four-course certificate program on AI in higher education for a fee of around $500. Aurora University (auora.edu) offers a certificate in "AI Ethics." Coursera (coursera.org) offers several certificate courses in AI and ethics from major universities including Michigan and Oxford that take from one to four months to complete. If Frank decides he wants to continue his college teaching program, he could become certificated and then begin offering ethics in AI courses that likely will bring in more students to his department and also bring in nonstudents who want professional credit. Any AI program his university initiates will likely include ethics courses that Frank will be asked to teach. That's one way to make Frank indispensable.

If Frank has aspirations for an administrative position, he might decide to investigate the Digital Educational Council (digitaleducationalcouncil.com) because it offers a 20-hour credential specifically on issues associated with AI in higher education, including a course in implementing AI in higher educational institutions.

What happens if Frank decides he wants to leave the university? Once he credentials himself to tie his knowledge of philosophy and ethics to knowledge of AI and ethics, he could pursue nonacademic positions. Many Fortune 500 companies are beginning to realize they need someone in charge of the ethical use of their AI tools. He could pursue a position as an AI ethicist, a compliance officer, or a policy adviser. Recently ZipRecruiter listed more than 60 jobs linked to AI and ethics, and no doubt the list will be growing.

Moving from Finance to AI Fintech Developer

The magic formula for marrying your current industry job with an AI-related job is to explore some of the future job trends and find careers that will leverage your existing expertise with a credential program that fills in the missing gaps in your education. Take an AI Fintech Developer position. Let's assume you already have extensive experience in the financial industry but fear the inroads of AI. Someone starting from scratch would find learning enough finance to be a useful challenge, but you already have a degree in finance and lots of experience. So, what do AI Fintech Developers do? The design and implement AI solutions for financial technology applications in a number of areas including fraud detection, credit scoring, and financial planning. You would want to fill in your AI educational gaps by picking up courses in machine learning and programming Python or Java.

From English Teacher to AI Literary Specialist

Let's say you're a high school English teacher. You even have earned your master's degree in literature, but you wonder how you can become part of the AI workforce and stop spending long evenings grading essays. It turns out there is a position titled Literature Specialist that is responsible for helping to train large language model AIs. To be eligible, candidates are expected to be an avid reader familiar with classical literature, modern and contemporary fiction, poetry, and critical analysis. They will challenge advanced language models on such things as thematic interpretation, narrative structure, authorial style, symbolism, and close reading. They'll document failure modes so the AI can be strengthened. They also evaluate the depth and validity of literary analysis, capture reproducible error traces and provide structured feedback.

Spotlight on a Career Changer

From Mid-Level Marketing Manager to AI-Enabled VP of Marketing

Marnel worked in marketing for a midsized company. He was terrified that AI would take away his job. When his CEO held a companywide meeting and announced that he wanted to integrate AI into all the company's processes, Marnel was terrified. He worried that this announcement meant he would be replaced by AI. When he was under enormous pressure to finish a marketing campaign on time, his boss called him in and said he needed to use AI to help with the campaign. Marnel's IT team gave him a crash course on AI tools the company had. The IT department had already integrated AI to help analyze customer behavior. To his surprise, AI actually enhanced Marnel's job. Faced with a deadline for his presentation, Marcel used AI to visualize his data to give him insight. His bosses were impressed with his presentation because it was backed up with solid data. Marcel began using more and more AI tools. The result was that Marcel was promoted to Director of Marketing.[4]

Linguist to AI Trainer

Wondering what to do with your degree in Linguistics? Believe it or not AI companies want linguists—those with degrees in linguistics—to train AI models. Applicants are told that if hired they will work to train AI models helping them understand and generate humanlike text that teaches AI reasoning, logic accuracy, nuance, and clarity. They help train AI models, helping the AI understand and generate humanlike text. An AI Trainer has to teach the AI reasoning and clarity.

Lateral Career Moves

Often the best career decision is to take your existing skills and job experiences, add an AI set of tailored courses and certificates and do the same essential job, but one with a lot more growth potential because of the expected growth of jobs that require a knowledge of AI.[5] Let's say you are a successful account executive selling various lab equipment to the university community, but you want to become part of the AI industry because you see it as a place where you can grow. Recently NVIDIA advertised for a senior account executive to sell to the university community. If you enhance your successful sales career experience with an AI credential, you would be well qualified for such a position. In fact, if you are a salesperson who uses Salesforce software, then a new AI certification might be perfect (https://trailhead.salesforce.com/agentblazer). No one expects the demand for AI products to decrease any time in the near future. Certainly, another example might be an experienced product manager who gains a knowledge of AI and becomes an AI product manager. Similarly, software engineers need to think seriously about their career prospects since AI now can write code. The key is knowing the right prompts to feed a generative AI tool. One logical transition is from software engineer to Prompt Engineer or Prompt Developer. Think about it. Smaller companies in particular will not have the expertise to work with generative AI. The courses listed below will help bridge the gap in skills.[6] Another example of a lateral transition is to go from someone with the Business Analyst title to an AI Business Analyst, someone who uses AI prompts as part of their decision making.

Similarly, people in quality assurance and project management positions would be well advised to learn about how they can use generative AI prompts and analysis in their decisions. Here are some other examples of possible lateral moves after validating AI knowledge through certifications:

- Auditor to certificated AI Auditor (ISACA Advanced in AI Audit [AAIA] Certificate)
- Project Manager to certificated AI Project Manager (PMI Certified Professional in Managing AI [PMI-CPMAI])
- Product Manager to AI certificated Product Manager (IBM AI Product Manager Professional Certificate through Coursera)
- Account Executive to AI Certificated Account Executive (Agent-Blazer certificated for Salesforce)
- Quality Assurance Engineer to AI certificated Quality Assurance Engineer (ISTQB® AI Testing Certification)
- Business Analyst to certificated AI Business Analyst (IBM certificate in Generative AI for Business Intelligence [BI] Analysts Specialization offered through Coursera)
- Software Developer to AI Engineer (AI Certificate Engineering Professional certificate)
- Supply Chain Specialist to AI Certificate Supply Chain Specialist (ChatGPT/Generative AI for Supply Chain Masterclass through Udemy.com)
- Business Intelligence Analyst to AI Certificated Business Intelligence Analyst (Generative AI for BI Analysts Specialization IBM course through Coursera)

Getting Up To Speed with Generative AI

College students today are using generative AI in their classes, so someone who has been part of the world of work for several years probably has not had the opportunity to pick up this knowledge. Still, it is far easier to pick up this information than for a college student to learn what took you years to learn on the job.[7] So, let's look at some programs to become comfortable with the world of generative AI. Johns Hopkins offers an online certificate program in Applied Generative AI that is worth investigating. (https://online.lifelonglearning.jhu.edu/jhu-certificate-program-applied-generative-ai) Educative (educative.io) offers an AI Essentials certificate program that has received positive reviews. If you enjoy watching Master Class, it has three episodes on "Achieve More with Generative AI." My Great Learning (mygreatlearning.com) has a free three-hour course in generative AI that comes with a certificate of completion.

The Appendix at the end of this book provides a list of online AI certificates in alphabetical order. Coursera (Coursera.org) offers courses and certificates in generative AI from IBM and Google as well as from several universities. It has a very well-received beginning course titled Generative AI for Everyone that might be a good starting point. These are video courses available online that are free or very low cost. There are additional fees to purchase the certificates after successfully completing the courses. Udemy (Udemy.com) offers a certificate program (Certificate in Generative AI Specialist) that should boost careers. IBM has an AI Product Manager certificate (Coursera.org). Google also offers a Google AI Professional Certificate on Coursera as well as an AI Essentials course. (https://grow.google/ai-essentials/). If you have experience with Microsoft products, then Microsoft's Generative AI certificate might be a valuable add-on (https://learn.microsoft.com/en-us/training/paths/introduction-to-ai-on-azure/). The Chartered Institute of Professional Certifications offers a Certificated Generative AI Specialist program (https://charteredcertifications.com/learning/courses/cgai) This program covers the principles of generative AI, data acquisition and preprocessing, natural language processing, creative AI applications, and so on. NVIDIA has its own NVIDIA-Certificated Associate—Generative AI LLMs program (https://www.nvidia.com/en-us/learn/certificateication/generative-ai-llm-associate/) which provides participants with knowledge in developing, integrating, and managing AI-driven applications utilizing generative AI and large language models (LLMs) with NVIDIA solutions. Anthropic offers several courses and certificates for people using Claude, its generative AI (https://www.anthropic.com/learn/claude-for-work).

What About Diving into an AI Career?

The emphasis so far in this chapter has been to focus on lateral moves for people who believe they will have greater growth and security career-wise by leveraging their current skills with AI-related certificates in their field. What about those people who want to dive into the deep waters of AI and do a complete change from their existing career. One expert lists these AI jobs as having the greatest growth opportunities in the future. Be warned though, these jobs require a good deal of additional education so you likely will have to earn one or more certificates. One option of course consists of certificate programs offered by community colleges. Here is a list of the top 10 highest paying AI jobs and salaries in 2026[8]:

- Machine Learning Engineer
- AI Engineer
- Data Scientist (Career interview with a data scientist) https://vault.com/videos/data-scientist
- Computer Vision Engineer (Learn more at opencv.org)
- Natural Language Processing Engineer
- Deep Learning Engineer
- AI Research Scientist
- Business Development Manager
- AI Product Manager
- AI Consultant

Your Local Community College Could Help

There are times when an online credential might not fill in all the gaps in your education. That's the time to look at what credentials your local community college offers. It might require a year of taking classes part-time at night, but the result could be well worth the effort. Take a position like a machine learning engineer. Maricopa Community College offers "Artificial Intelligence and Machine Learning," a certificate program. Requiring 21 to 36 units, students learn to build machine learning models that can be used for predicting, making decisions and enhancing human capabilities. It provides an introduction to AI and machine learning, natural language processing, computer vision, and AI for business solutions and other applications. The college points out that the skills learned in this program can be used in "the information technology, automotive, healthcare, aerospace, industrial, and manufacturing industries." Students' coursework includes classes in computer programming, math, and statistics.

Let's look at a second example. Mount San Antonio College offers classes in person or online. Its Big Data certificate program requires three courses that prepare a student in the areas of data science, data analysis, Big Data, and data mining.

Filling in Gaps

Notice how the Maricopa County Community College credential covers so many of the skills generally acknowledged to be required to become an AI professional including programming, math and statistics. So, even if you do not live near a community college that offers such a comprehensive credential, you can study the actual courses offered and piece together a couple of credentials plus some math, statistics, and programming classes to fill in gaps in your knowledge portfolio.

Conclusion

If you decide that rather than try to flee your current job and career path because of a fear of AI you prefer to modify your career path to include AI, then you have two choices. If you already are skilled in a profession such as education project management, auditing, or finance, you can pursue a lateral move by filling in the gaps in your knowledge of AI with credentials that will validate your ability to use AI in your job. That way you can become a leader in your company's use of AI. If you feel that you need to change careers and want a career that incorporates AI, then you need to use tools described in Chapter 4 to identify your strengths and interests and then zero in on an AI-related career. Buttressed by your transferable skills, you can then use the Appendix in this book to identify credentials that can help you qualify for an AI-related position. The beauty of the credentials listed in the Appendix is that they are video based so that you can take these classes at home in your spare time. If you are able to devote full time to your career makeover, then obviously the time required to earn these credentials will be much shorter.

CHAPTER 4

Learn Your Real Strengths, Capabilities, and Interests

Most of us fall into a career without much thought. We graduate school, get a job, and then rarely think how well it really matches our interests and aptitudes. Is the job perfect? Likely it is not and we may experience some discontent, but generally a feeling of inertia causes us to persevere until we are faced with a crisis such as being laid off or fired. So, now is the time for you to consider a number of different tests. There just might be a career path out there that more closely matches your profile and offers a chance for growth without the impending doom that AI will destroy.

The Motivational Appraisal of Personal Potential Test

Who would think a 20-minute, 71-question test could provide so much information? Designed to analyze your motivations and personal preferences, the Motivational Appraisal of Personal Potential (MAPP) test provides you with information on the time of tasks you want to perform. Do you enjoy working with people or do you prefer working alone? What kinds of tools do you enjoy using? What kind of routine do you prefer for your job? How important is creativity in the job you want to perform? Do you prefer working with machines? Do you require a job that has lots of variety?

While several firms offer the MAPP test online with assessments for a fee, be wary because many of these companies are really selling career coaching and job matching. Alumni often can contact their university career center and schedule the test; sometimes there is a modest fee. If you are not eligible, you can take the test online generally for a fee ranging from $90 to $150, depending on the degree of assessment you want. A 30-page in-depth analysis for $150 probably is worth it because of the wealth of information it provides.

The O*NET Interest Profiler

Sponsored by the U.S. Department of Labor, this free, 60-question test maps interests to over 900 occupations. This free test matches you to occupations based on whether you are Realistic, Investigative, Artistic, Social, Enterprising, or Conventional. You can take a 30-question version online (https://onetinterestprofiler.org) or the 60-question version (https://www.mynextmove.org/explore/ip?client=eccc). The longer version only takes about 20 minutes to complete. Chapter 7 of the online technical manual provides linkage to occupations that match your profile.[1]

My Next Move

My Next Move (mynextmove.org) offers the O*NET Interest Profiler, but it adds some other features that make it worthwhile visiting. It lists careers sorted by your interests, a list of careers with "bright outlooks," information about job preparation, and an apprentice job finder. Thus, if you have already determined you want to go into a blue-collar profession that requires an apprenticeship, this link allows you to find apprenticeship jobs by typing in specific zip codes.

Career Explorer

Career Explorer (careerexplorer.com) offers an aptitude test that has received rave reviews. It also offers another way to match your skills and aptitudes as well as your personality and past work history with jobs. The site offers an enormous number of job titles. If one fascinates you, clicking on it will bring up the requirements, the skills required, the salary, and other key information.

The Myers-Briggs Type Indicator

The MBTI is a personality test that helps applicants learn more about themselves, including what work styles they flourish in and what kinds of people they work most effectively with. The company that sells the test offers a sample report to show the kinds of information that you might find helpful.[2] It is possible that your college placement center might offer the test free or at a reasonable price for alumni. Equally important, that placement center might make a career counselor available who can help you understand what your profile means and what kinds of jobs and careers might best match with your personality and interests. If you cannot use your college placement center, the test can be purchased and taken online for around $80.[3]

The 16 Personalities Test

The 16 Personalities (www.16personalitiestest.com) is a free variant of the MBTI Test. It offers valuable information to help explain what the test results actually mean and how these results correspond to various jobs and careers.

The Strong Interest Inventory Assessment

This test is very well respected. It takes about 40 minutes and must be administered by someone who is trained and credentialed in this test. Your best bet is asking a university career center if they offer it. Questions cover various activities and occupations, your leisure activities, preferred work environment, and so on. The results categorize you in six general occupational themes.

The test is usually abbreviated as RIASEC to cover Realistic, Investigative, Artistic, Social, Enterprising, and Conventional. You can score high in two or even three related themes. You will receive a report that reveals information about what work style you prefer, your interests, and what occupations match up most closely with your scores. Here is a link to an excellent description of the test.[4]

Career Fitter

Career Fitter (https://www.careerfitter.com) offers a free 60-question aptitude test that you then can use to match your profile with more than 1,000 occupations. The Resources section enables you to look at salary ranges, educational requirements, and growth prospects for a specific occupation.

This website (https://www.mynextmove.org) offers an aptitude test, an option to browse possible careers, and even a place for you to list keywords that describe your ideal career which the website will then match with possible occupations. Equally important, this website allows you to search for apprenticeships for blue-collar professions.

Job Test

This aptitude test takes around 20 minutes, and its website offers a directory of career coaches. This test does cost money depending upon the degree of analysis you want. It is the CAPBOI personality model, which uses AI to match six key personality traits—Communal, Analytical, Communal, Pragmatic, Bold and Orthodox, and Imaginative—with various occupations.[5]

Spotlight on a Career Changer

From a Career in Retail to an Urban Planner Via Retraining

Kate Portillo went back to school to train for a career in urban planning after 13 years as a manager in the retail industry. She made the change at midlife with her children in elementary school after finding a mentor to guide her. She voluntarily worked on her condo board and found she loved working on all the processes associated with major improvement projects. She began a master's degree in urban planning at 42 years of age. She graduated and found a job as a planning manager.[6]

Summarizing What You Know About Yourself

Once you've taken some of these tests and received the reports analyzing the results, you should be able to get a better idea about what you like and dislike. Let's look at some categories.

Work Environment

The tests you took probed to find what you liked and disliked about the various work environments where you've worked. If some of these questions weren't addressed in your tests, now is the time to consider them:

- Do you prefer close supervision or a lot of freedom in your daily work life?
- Do you prefer a career where you feel you are helping others?
- Do you prefer working for a nonprofit?
- Do you prefer working in teams or working alone?
- Do you thrive in a pressure environment or prefer a more relaxed environment?
- Do you want to work in an environment where you are able to make decisions?
- Is it important to you to be regarded as an expert in your field?
- Is it important to you to work in a "secure" environment where there is little turnover?
- Do you want to be in charge or can you work for others without second-guessing them?
- Is it important to you that your job permits you to use your creativity?
- Is it important to you to work remotely or do you prefer a hybrid mix of office and home?
- Are you adaptable enough to work in a fast-changing office environment?
- Do you prefer to work with machines rather than with people?
- Do you prefer a strict eight-hour work day or are you willing to work longer and on weekends when the job requires it?
- Do you have a minimum salary in mind?
- Do you want a salaried position with benefits or prefer a high fee as an independent contractor?
- How willing are you to commute or relocate?

Personal Traits

You can use some of the tools the test websites offer to match your personal traits with careers and specific jobs by typing in some of these traits and looking for matches:

- Are you analytical? Do you prefer that kind of work?
- Are you a loner or do you prefer a social environment at work?
- Do you want a position where you can use your organizational skills?
- Do you want a position where you can manage or supervise others?
- Do you have the empathy and diplomatic skills to deal with difficult people?

The point is that you should have an idea of what your personal traits and attitudes toward different types of work environment are. The next step in learning about yourself is to analyze all of your past work and voluntary positions and look to see what skills you exhibited that will be transferable to a new career and job.

Determining Your Transferable Skills

Once you know what careers most closely match your interests and aptitudes, the next question you should ask yourself is what your transferable skills are. Since you are in the process of changing careers, it is now time to take a long walk down memory lane and think very carefully about your past jobs. Also think of any volunteer work you did whether it was for the Cub Scouts, Brownies, your church or other religious organization, service organizations, and so on. Did you coach children's sports teams? What tasks did you perform? Are there examples where you went far beyond the job requirements to complete a task? Are any of your accomplishments quantifiable? If so, jot that information down because you'll need it later when you put together a resume designed specifically for a job in your new career area.

One way to analyze your past experiences as well as prepare for writing your resume and preparing for interviews is to use the STAR method. For your key experiences, define the **S**ituation, **T**ask, **A**ction, and **R**esult. This helps identify the specific, transferable, or portable skill used in that situation.[7]

The Divide Between Hard and Soft Transferable Skills

"Hard skills" are very easy to quantify and easy to see if they are transferable to a new job and career because a job posting will indicate, for example, that the applicant has to be able to code in C++. Either the applicant can demonstrate that capability or he or she can't by pointing to courses or training taken or actual programming performed for a specific job. Another "hard skill" often required is a knowledge of Microsoft Office, perhaps with an emphasis on Excel if it is a financial position or PowerPoint if it is a management or sales position. If you haven't used your Microsoft Office skills in your various jobs but did so in your voluntary positions, be sure to list those experiences. A simple test can help an employer determine whether you have this hard skill or not. Knowledge of a foreign language is another example of a hard transferable skill. Often companies can test applicants' knowledge of "hard" skills rather easily. Either an applicant can demonstrate an ability to read or speak in Spanish or he cannot. Either the applicant can explain how to solve a problem by creating a database or they cannot. "Hard" skills are much easier to identify than soft skills because a job title rarely reflects the soft skills required.

Soft skills are more difficult to document since a job title or description might not contain key terms associated with soft transferable skills. Still, according to the Pew Research Center, jobs requiring strong "soft" skills, such as interpersonal, management and communication, have grown 83 percent over the last 30 years.[8] Let's examine some soft skills that definitely are transferable from one job and career to another. Let's say you think of yourself at your previous job as an **organized** person. Someone might even have commented about how organized you were. What are some ways you demonstrated being organized? Did you have to **prioritize** tasks? Did your job require great **attention to detail**? Did you have to **budget** carefully? Did you have to demonstrate **project management** skills by handling a project from start to finish? I remember the first time I was given a budget to balance. I worked night and day and told my boss I was really close to balancing the books. "Close isn't good enough," he said, and I knew I had to do better.

Communications skills are pretty easy to recognize. Did you have to **communicate** with customers in previous jobs? Did you have to **give presentations**? Did you do **internal training** sessions for your fellow employees? Did you **write** press releases or perhaps internal and/or external reports? Were you ever required to **edit** other employees' written work? Did you write a newsletter for your company or in one of your voluntary positions? Did you write a blog?

Analytical Skills usually are associated with positions like data analyst, but these soft skills can be found in a variety of jobs. Did you have to do any **problem solving** in your jobs? Did you have to do **research** to find the best solution to a problem? Did you have to tackle a very complex problem that required very careful **analysis** and **planning** to solve? Did you have to **analyze** market research **data** or sales data and come to conclusions?

Leadership skills sound like they would be so easy to identify, but what if your job titles did not specifically identify you as a leader? Did you have to **resolve conflicts** in your department? Were you expected to engage in team building for your group? Did you have to **delegate** certain tasks to others and persuade them to agree to do them? Can you point to people you have **mentored** who were successful? Were you responsible for **leading others** in meeting a specific goal? I once received a promotion for leading my group to complete what at first glance seemed like an impossible goal to achieve. It wasn't explicit in my job description, but the company considered it important because the goal was issued by our parent company and our President was desperate for his recently acquired company to look as good as possible.

Creativity is another soft skill that requires some thought to identify. Potential employers often will ask if you ever were required to think "outside the box" to solve a specific problem. One time I was in charge of fund raising for my religious institution. I promised that I would find a way to meet expenses. What could I do? I visited a Catholic Church and noticed how successful it was with its Bingo games. I started Bingo and had the women's auxiliary bake sweets to sell to the Bingo players. Bingo was an enormous success. How about another example? I know one individual who found that the government had issued some new regulations that made it impossible for his company to continue to do business as usual. Over the weekend he brooded and thought about the situation and developed a brand-new way for his company to run its business. That's thinking outside the box!

Often you can identify your creativity on the job without having been in a leadership position. Did you develop a new marketing campaign? Did you find a way to change the company's supply chain to make your company's products more profitable? Perhaps you created a new logo for your company or used creative problem solving to make your team work more efficiently. Did you come up with a new use or new market for a product that no longer was selling?

Interpersonal skills can be found in all kinds of jobs. Did you have to work with a team? Did you have to confront an employee to diplomatically discuss a touchy subject and get him or her to agree to change behavior? Was there a situation that required you to network successfully with vendors or even competitors? Was there some kind of tragedy in one of your places of work that required you not only to show diplomatic skills but also empathy?

There are all kinds of verbs that describe soft skills. They clearly become even more attractive to a potential employer if you can quantify them. So, for example, if you can point out that your motivation campaign resulted in a 20 percent increase in sales, you've made the case for that skill. Here is a far-from-complete list of verbs describing soft skills for you to consider when thinking about your past jobs and volunteer efforts[9]:

- Organize
- Persuade
- Research
- Supervise
- Train
- Analyze
- Lead
- Manage
- Demonstrate flexibility
- Take initiative
- Negotiate
- Mentor
- Collaborate
- Work independently
- Manage time
- Plan

Depending on your job history, it might help you to compare your tasks with a different way of viewing your transferable skills:

Communication Skills

- Write
- Edit
- Present
- Train
- Publish newsletter

Data Skills

- Organize
- Analyze
- Plan
- Compile
- Research
- Classify

Interpersonal Skills

- Negotiate
- Lead team
- Collaborate
- Sell
- Persuade

Management Skills

- Lead
- Supervise
- Achieve
- Build
- Direct
- Delegate
- Motivate
- Mediate
- Evaluate
- Expand
- Develop

Conclusion

This chapter is really a chapter in self-discovery. How can you write a decent cover letter and resume or interview for a position if you don't know enough about your transferable skills to convince an employer that you don't need to step way back on a salary schedule? Once you take the various aptitude tests, you will probably find the analysis reports from the test websites to be surprising. You also might be surprised how many transferable skills you can discover by combining your work and volunteer positions. As an example, I came to the conclusion that my major strengths were a combination of analytical and communications skills. I used my speaking and writing skills as a law enforcement administrator tasked with writing a major report each year, a technical trainer, a technical writer, an English professor, computer science professor, a computer salesman, a Fuller Brush salesman, and a research director. I used my analytical skills *and* communications skills as a network manager and as an industry analyst. These skills did not turn out to be that helpful, though, when I was an autopsy assistant since I worked mostly with the dead.

In the next chapter we'll examine several careers that should hold up well against the onslaught of AI. The tools you learned to use in this chapter will help you match your skills and interests and see which ones are possible matches.

CHAPTER 5

Explore Careers Likely to Survive AI and Robots

The first point I want to make once again is that you will probably change jobs and careers several times because you will need to stay agile as AI becomes more capable of performing various tasks. The good news is that after a period of adjustment AI is likely to also create the need for some new careers. On that point I'm much more optimistic than Elon Musk who thinks no one will need to work in a few years. In this chapter I've avoided for the most part listing careers that require advanced degrees because the point of this book is that it is possible to make lateral career moves using certificates as a quick way to qualify yourself. The exceptions to this rule are the skilled trade careers discussed later.

Notice I've added robots to the threat to many jobs because AI added to robots means they can start to do mobile tasks. We're already seeing this trend. Amazon is replacing its warehouse workers with robots, and smarter robots are on the horizon. Unlike Elon Musk, however, I do not believe we will see robots with AI capabilities that can perform ALL jobs humans can perform within five years. Perhaps the best way to survey jobs and careers likely to survive AI and robots is to categorize them. Keep in mind as a general rule, the more human interaction a job or career requires, the less likely it is going to be completely replaced by AI and/or robots.

Cognizant, an IT consulting company, did a study of the percentage of a job's tasks AI is likely to be able to perform. At the high-end were Financial Managers (84 percent) and Office and Administrative Support (60 percent to 68 percent). At the lower end were the following jobs[1]:

- Construction 12 percent impacted
- Mechanics 17 percent impacted
- Installation and Repair 20 percent impacted

- Protective Services (police, guards) 20 percent to 29 percent impacted
- Personal Care Roles (childcare, elder care, etc.) 20 percent to 29 percent impacted
- Health care support roles 29 percent impacted

The general consensus of experts is that jobs that require empathy, human judgment, creativity, and human dexterity as well as the ability to make complex decisions will continue to require humans. One expert summarized the skills required for jobs AI cannot do this way[2]:

- Emotional Intelligence and Empathy: Understanding feelings, resolving tension, and 1. offering human comfort.
- Complex Physical Dexterity: Real time adaptation, fine motor control, and tactile judgment.
- Creative Vision and Cultural Taste: Creating new ideas, shaping culture, and setting direction.
- Ethical Judgment and Moral Reasoning: Making decisions with values, responsibility, and context.
- Strategic Improvisation: Responding to new situations without scripts.
- Trust Building and Relationship Capital: Earning credibility through presence and lived experience.
- Contextual Integration: Synthesizing signals, reading dynamics, and adjusting in the moment.

Health Care

While no one can ever accuse the health care industry of not generating a lot of paper, it is the people, the patients, that require human interaction. Those careers and jobs should be relatively safe from automation.[3]

Nurses will have to learn about AI because they will be working in conjunction with it in the near future. It is not hard to see robots capable of administering shots for example. Doctors and physician assistants are likely to keep their jobs because people prefer to talk with humans when it comes to their health. That doesn't mean doctors won't be using AI though. AIs can already read x-rays better than radiologists, and they can look at symptoms and make educated guesses for a diagnosis, but patients want to talk to a human radiologist when it comes to treatment options. We will need anesthesiology technicians, x-ray technicians, diagnostic medical sonographers, MRI technologists, radiation therapists,[4] lab technicians, and so on. Health care also will create all kinds of positions for management positions. The Appendix lists a number of fascinating online certificates in various areas of health care.

Remember that the key is to look at health care jobs that have direct contact with other people. HR professionals will still be needed as will physical therapists, respiratory therapists, nutritionists, dieticians, mental health counselors, occupational therapists, medical assistants, patient care specialists, phlebotomy technicians, ECG technicians, and so on. Outside of the hospital there will continue to be a need for drug counselors, psychologists, vocational counselors, exercise coaches, and even life coaches.[5]

Telemedicine will be expanding, and AI will be part of this expansion, but there will be a need for medical technicians to work with AI tools.[6] Robots equipped with AI are likely to play many roles in a hospital including delivering drugs from one location to another, security in urban hospitals, and assisting in procedures such as nuclear medicine where radioactivity exposure might be a factor. The point is that, no matter how smart these robots are, they will create the need for humans to perform supportive roles. Someone will need to maintain and repair the robots. Other people will need to procure the robots and to train staff how to work with the robots. Some humans will be required to sell robots to hospitals while others will need to deliver them.

Health care is one industry where Big Data is everywhere. There will continue to be jobs for people such as data analysts and data scientists. There also will be a need for people responsible for the ethical use of AI in a medical facility. The health care facilities will continue to need people to run its infrastructures including network managers, cybersecurity experts, and facility managers.

If you've been to a dentist or a veterinarian lately, you'll remember how important it was to have a human dental hygienist and dental assistant as well as a human veterinarian assistant to care for your pet. In the Appendix you will even find online programs to train as a veterinary assistant. When it comes to sprucing up your pet, you likely will want a human person to groom and bathe Fido. Should you need to take a trip, you'll want humans to care for your pet. We can extend the list of human service jobs. I've mentioned a few types of jobs that directly touch humans. We can add others such as aestheticians, salon stylists, and elderly support workers.

Education

Education positions from preschool through high school will continue to be available, especially for those teachers who certify themselves in programs to help them work along-side AI tools. Education careers include positions in training of various types, from technology training to business and leadership training positions. I've been at technical training and business training positions, and I can't imagine them ever being replaced entirely by AI, although I can see those positions working in conjunction with AI tutors. Think outside the box. A study of jobs least likely to be impact by AI includes music therapists and art therapists.[7]

Creative Jobs

If you have a creative bent, then you can find a comfortable niche where AI will not threaten your livelihood. If you paint, weave, create music or jewelry, or anyone of a hundred other artistic sub specialties, you'll be safe. That also includes all the people who support these creative fields as well as people in the dramatic arts. One interesting forecast is that when governments decide to provide a basic income for people who have lost their jobs to AI, many people will spend more and more time in virtual immersive worlds. Someone will need to create these worlds. The one element missing from AI is creativity. That quality extends to entrepreneurship. Small businesses are likely to spring up as a result of human ingenuity, and of course chefs will likely not be replaced by smart robots.

The Legal Profession

We will still need lawyers, paralegals, and judges. In fact, there are bound to be at least two new types of specializations for lawyers in the near future. AI is bound to create legal issues as are robots. What if a robot inadvertently injures someone? Who is responsible? Similarly, what if an AI creates a situation where someone is hurt?

Emergency Workers and Criminal Justice

We don't call a robot when we see a fire or when a loved one is injured. We'll need firefighters as well as all the support staff around them. We'll need paramedics and emergency medical technicians (EMTs) as well as their support staff as well. Public-funded criminal justice positions will also be available. Don't just think of police officers, but think of all the ancillary positions—CSI technician, DNA technicians, and others. I've worked as a civilian employee in a large urban police department, and I can tell you that there are all kinds of positions for civilians who never carry a gun or chase the bad guys.

Environmental Workers

Despite the current administration's focus on oil, we will need people in sustainability energy fields such as wind and solar. Green jobs are likely to continue to grow. We already have far more people working in solar energy than in the coal industry. I coauthored a book a few years ago: *Paint Your Career Green*, which listed the hundreds of jobs associated with green technology. Community colleges offer a number of certificates in various types of green technology. Remember this industry is far broader than most people realize. There are jobs in creating sustainable food, water management, geothermal technology, LEED (Leadership in Energy and Environmental Design) construction, even green real estate. There also will be a need for green policy experts, advocates, sales people, trainers, technicians, and so on. Because green industries are still relatively young, it is possible to earn a certificate and use your transferable skills to make a lateral move to jobs and careers without taking a major pay cut. A building contractor, for example, can add a LEED certification and an architect can add a green certificate and focus on designing green buildings.

The Human Element for Computer-Centric Jobs

Once again, no office worker having computer problems wants to talk with an AI tool. The computer support desk is a safe haven, although support staff will have to learn to use AI tools in their work. Similarly, one of the real growth areas is cybersecurity. This book's Appendix lists a number of cybersecurity certificates that can be earned completely online. Security will become more and not less important in the future. Additional specializations are appearing that offer opportunities for career growth including forensic cybersecurity, the knowledge to do detective work to uncover what the bad guys are doing online.

Business Growth Areas

People will still need financial advisers to help them with their investments even though those same advisers are likely to be using AI tools to weigh investment options. Various types of marketing positions will continue to grow, especially social media marketing and digital marketing of all types. One expert recently pointed to several high-growth areas of marketing where people will make use of AI tools including: Reach (including inbound techniques), Programmatic Media Buying, Propensity Modeling, Predictive Analytics, and Dynamic Pricing.[8]

Add sales to jobs with high-growth potential that are AI-resistant. The Appendix offers several options for certificates in those areas. Forecasts includes robust growth for operations managers, engagement managers, management analysts, and market research managers.[9]

Skilled Trades

The good news is that the demand for people in the skilled trades is growing because of aging infrastructure and a dwindling supply of aging workers. Community colleges and high schools began eliminating their skilled trades programs including auto shop training several years ago. Who would have guessed that these vocational areas are now in high demand as people realize that a college degree is no longer a magic ticket to high-salary jobs. In fact, salaries and demand

Spotlight on a Career Changer

From Advertising and Media to Artist and Designer

Harriet Hoult had been in the advertising/media field as a project manager when she took a break from work. Rather than return, she decided to give notice because she no longer felt any motivation for her previous job. One key question she asked herself is what she would do if she only had a year left to live. The answer was full-time artist and designer. She took classes, read books, and listened to podcasts on her new career choice while supporting herself in freelance roles using her previous job experience. She now has had her studio for 10 years and is very happy.[10]

are both increasing for skilled workers. If you scored high on your interest and aptitude for working with machines, it is definitely a career option worth considering because many of these trades actually pay while you train as an apprentice. While the majority of this book focuses on certificates available online for a career change, it is clear that you need hands-on training to work in the skilled trades. No one wants someone coming to fix an air conditioner, a toilet, or an electrical problem if they have only taken online classes without any hands-on experience.

One place to start is to look up the various skilled trades discussed below in the O-NET Online (onetonline.org). Here you will find a list of job titles associated with the profession. You'll see a list of tasks performed as well as several other sections including:

- Technology Skills
- Work Activities
- Detailed Work Activities
- Work Content (by percentage of time each day)
- Experience Required
- Training and Credentials (You can select state and zip code for local training and credentials)
- Apprenticeship Opportunities

What about what knowledge and skills you need to bring to the work? The O-NET online tells you in the following sections:

- Worker Requirements
- Knowledge
- Education
- Worker Characteristics: Abilities
- Worker Characteristics: Interests
- Work Styles

You also will find basic information on pay (by state) as well as employment trends. In addition, you will find sections on:

- Job Openings on the Web (by state or zip code)
- Related Occupations
- National Associations
- Accreditation, Certification, and Unions

Keep in mind that the skilled trades described below offer many support positions as well including customer relations, sales, and management.

Electrician as a Career Option

There are a number of different paths that can lead to a career as an electrician. The basic starting point is a high school diploma or equivalent. One way to start is with a good electrician course; this first class can be taken online. While trade schools offer this course, so do a number of community colleges. The trade-off is that the trade school's program is likely to be faster to complete but more expensive. Another way is to skip that step and find an apprenticeship program and work with an experienced electrician. Apprenticeship programs last around four years, but you will receive pay and benefits during that time. You work full time during the day and then go to class at night once a week or online. Key apprenticeship paths include the union—IBEW/NECA, often through the Electrical Training Institute (ETI) or Joint Apprenticeship and Training Committee (JATC). These programs offer comprehensive training and benefits.

There are also non-Union/Merit Shop (Independent Electrical Contractors [IEC], Associated Builders and Contractors [ABC], Western Electrical Contractors Association [WECA]) training. The IEC or ABC offers training. In California, as an example, the WECA offers commercial, residential, and low-voltage apprenticeships. Common apprenticeships offered include Inside Wireman—working on commercial and industrial electrical installation and Residential Wireman—working on residential electrical systems. In any event, after your apprenticeship you will move up your career ladder and become journeyman and later a master electrician. Some electricians suggest that joining a union program makes a lot of sense if you are relatively young because of the retirement options over 20 to 30 years. The argument for not joining a union is that you have more flexibility so that you do not have to wait until a union job becomes available.

Plumber as a Career Option

In some ways the career path toward a plumbing career is similar to that of an electrician. Your initial decision is whether to take a program in plumbing at a trade school or community college or to start with a plumbing apprenticeship program. Obviously, you are a step ahead if you have the initial training before looking for an apprenticeship program under the supervision of a master plumber. It takes anywhere from two to five years to complete your apprenticeship depending on how many hours you accumulate before you can take the licensing exam. The next step is to become a journeyman plumber. At that point you no longer have to work under the supervision of a master plumber. The final step after several years is to take a licensing exam and become a master plumber. After an apprenticeship, you will be able to take a licensing exam. These exams are state-specific. Pass the exam and you can start working as a residential electrician or electrician apprentice.

HVAC Technician as a Career Option

The *Occupational Outlook Handbook* indicates that HVAC (Heating, Ventilation, Air Conditioning, and Refrigeration) Mechanics and Installers are growing faster than average rate. As temperatures continue to rise, the job opportunities can only improve. Community colleges and trade schools do offer initial training before an apprenticeship, but some technicians opt to start an apprenticeship program immediately that can take three to five years. During this time apprentices receive hands-on training and classroom instruction while earning wages. They need to pass HVAC certification exams offered by organizations such as the North American Technician Excellence (NATE) (https/natex.org/) or the Refrigeration Service Engineers Society (RSES) (https//rses.org/). The U.S. Department of Labor has a website (apprenticeship.gov) and a phone number (877-872-5627) that will provide you with information on apprenticeship opportunities.[11]

Welding as a Career

Welding is a career that appears to be bullet-proof from major AI's inroads because while robots with AI can do routine jobs, they cannot do complex jobs.[12] It reveals that classroom training takes a year or less, and there are a number of approved apprenticeship programs in the following areas:

- Lead Burner
- Welder (Existing Title: Welder, Combination)
- Welder, Arc
- Welder, Combination
- Welder-Fitter

The government site appreticeships.gov provides information on specific apprenticeships. Career information is available from the American Welding Society as well as from the International Association of Machinists and Aerospace Workers, and the International Association of Bridge, Structural, Ornamental and Reinforcing Iron Workers. Certification is through the International Brotherhood of Boilermakers.

The career path begins for most applicants with schooling and an apprenticeship. Companies prefer applicants who have had some schooling. Advancement could include becoming a certificated welding inspector or even a project manager. Among the highest paid welders are those in scheduled air transportation and electric power generation, transmission, and distribution.

Automobile Technician as a Career Path

Community colleges and trade schools offer training for a career in automotive technology. Generally, technicians demonstrate their knowledge by passing tests and becoming accredited in such specific areas as brakes, engines, emissions, hybrids, EV (electric vehicle) systems, and electrical systems. Career paths include service technician with a path toward ultimately becoming a master technician, a diagnostic specialist, and more customer-facing positions such as a service manager, a parts manager or customer service representative.

Unlike some other skilled trades where apprenticeships are very much a part of the training, automobile repair centers do not want people to learn on the job. They prefer to hire people who have acquired their knowledge through an accredited program.

Conclusion

For those people who do not want AI to steal their jobs and careers, the answer is to focus on jobs and careers where human interaction is important, workers have to deal with complex situations that require human ingenuity, and/or complex physical challenges. Health care is one industry that offers a lot of high-paying jobs and careers that are people-centric, but there are other key industries that require human creativity and physical skills such as the skilled trades and the arts.

CHAPTER 6

Leveraging Social Media

A recruiter today talking to a job hunter might whisper one word of advice, "network." With social media, it is so much easier today to build up a social network that can help you reach the key decision makers or, at least, reach people who can reach the decision makers. At the very minimum, you can find people who at least can walk down the hall and tell an HR person to put your resume in the potential bucket of people to be considered for a position. In this chapter we'll look at ways you can use social media tools as well as develop mentors who can help you achieve your career goals.

First Things First: Your LinkedIn Profile

Before you start contacting people, it is imperative that you do some spring cleaning and get your LinkedIn profile in the best possible shape since it is the first thing potential recruiters or contacts will see. The latest statistics suggest that the new trend toward including a photo of yourself is accelerating with profiles with photos generating far more interest than those without them.[1]

Another portion of your LinkedIn profile often ignored or filled with stilted prose is the About section. Some recruiters say they look at the photo and then they look at the About section before checking to see if the profile contains keywords linked to their job description. One key ingredient that makes a summary or "About" section stand out for recruiters is for it to tell a story and to reveal something about yourself. The idea is to "hook" the recruiter with an interesting story narrated in the first person.[2] So, instead of simply summarizing yourself as a "Go-getter who exceeded all performance goals," perhaps you can start with something like this: "I was always the one who got invited to my clients' birthday parties ...."

Don't stop there, though, extol your qualifications, but make sure to be specific about the job you are seeking. If you have a specific title, that's even better if it matches the jobs you are applying for.

Remember, you are selling yourself as a product so describe yourself accordingly. Why should recruiters care? They might care, though, if your value proposition described yourself as an XYZ-certificated veteran project manager of the ABC industry who has always completed projects under budget and on time. One piece of advice from an expert is to try to craft a catchy headline that will catch a recruiter's attention.[3]

You need to go over your profile with a fine-tooth comb to catch any errors. Make sure that the name on your profile is the same as the one on your resume—Do not have Stan in one place and Stanley in the other. For geographic location, experts say to list the metropolitan area rather than a suburb because the metros appear more often in searches. Another useful suggestion is to use a short custom URL that is easy to remember, both for you and for potential recruiters.[4]

What about your job titles and skills sections? Make sure your job titles are the ones that most companies use and nothing so cute that it won't show up in a recruiter's search. You can put the company's cute title in parentheses if you wish. No one is going to be doing a search looking for "Chief Dream Maker" but they certainly might be doing one on "Creative Marketing Director."

Your skills section is critical and should reflect as many of the skills listed in the job descriptions you can find. Recruiters say it is useful to match skills with endorsements that describe those skills.[5]

Using AI to Help with Your LinkedIn Profile

You can use your generative AI to help craft your LinkedIn Profile. Tell it that it is playing the role of a recruiter for XYZ company (the one where you are applying). Ask it to analyze your Profile, indicate how you are perceived, and then rewrite it to attract recruiters. Of course, once AI writes something, you need to go over it and tweak it so that it doesn't sound like it was written by AI.

Adding Contacts to Your LinkedIn Account

I know you might have believed in only adding people who you thought you knew pretty well, but before you begin your big job-hunting campaign you want to beef-up your contact list. Why? The answer is that while the people you know casually and add might not help you hit the jackpot with a major connection, it is the second level contacts that opens up an entirely new world. Each person you add has the people they are directly connected to, but they also have the names of people who are directly connected to those people. The list of names grows quickly.

If you haven't talked to someone in quite a while, don't just send them a request to connect because they will likely ignore it. You should send them a note. Remind them of your history with them in the past and then ask for them to accept your invitation.[6]

The Power of LinkedIn Search Capabilities

Keep in mind that you are able to do a search on your first connections, those people connected to your first connections (second connections) and those connected to your second connections (or third connections). What good does that do you? Let's say you're in Sales and currently live in Miami or want to move there. You can begin by doing a search on the profile page of one of your first-level connections for VPs of Sales and Sales Managers and use the "All Filter" button to specify the Miami metropolitan area. You can also search for Sales Recruiters in the greater Miami metropolitan area. You can go through the list that comes up. If you are not a direct connection to these people, you can send them a message in which you explain who you are and tell them how pleased you would be to connect with them.[7]

When you do begin searching for jobs, you can utilize LinkedIn's search capabilities to search by criteria you set. You can turn on alerts for such jobs, indicate the frequency you want to receive alerts, and also set up alerts when jobs are posted by a specific company. You can set the toggle to off when you no longer want to receive alerts on a specific job search.[8]

If you pay for "Premium" on LinkedIn, you can use LinkedIn InMail instead of e-mail to reach people. The advantage of InMail is that it has a 10 percent to 25 percent response rate versus around 1 percent for regular e-mail, but it is limited to 50 e-mails a month.[9]

One of the problems with key people you need to contact is that often they do not list their e-mail addresses. One solution is to use hunter.io.[10] This site enables you to enter a person's name and their company's website to find or guess their professional e-mail address. One nice feature of this website is that you can do bulk e-mail address searches. Two other useful tools include Hotspot Sales and Crystal. Hotspot Sales will give you the power to know when and how often your e-mail recipients opened their e-mail from you and even what device they used, while Crystal provides you with a profile of a prospective employer you are cold e-mailing to and offers suggestions as to when to send the e-mail and the kind of approach that person prefers.[11]

When you do begin searching for jobs, you can utilize LinkedIn's search capabilities to search by criteria you set. You can turn on alerts for such jobs, indicate the frequency you want to receive alerts, and also set up alerts when jobs are posted by a specific company. You can set the toggle to off when you no longer want to receive alerts on a specific job search.[12]

In any event, research shows that if you keep your messages under 400 characters, you will generate 22 percent more responses, and if you include two specific details from their profile, you get a 15 percent higher engagement. Finally, try sending your e-mails on Monday for a quicker response and personalize your messages based on the person's background and interests.[13]

Identifying Allies Within a Company

You seem like a perfect candidate for a position with XYZ company, but you probably need some inside help. The solution is to use LinkedIn's search capabilities to look at the company page on LinkedIn. Just type in the company name in the search box. You then can search by job title, college alumni, and so on. You can see if any of these people are directly connected to you, or perhaps you have a second-degree contact who can introduce you. Don't forget to search for people who have worked at that company in the past, particularly those who were in the right department or held the job title you are applying for. You also can follow the company page. That might provide you with some key information about the company before an interview.[14]

Developing Contacts Through LinkedIn Groups

LinkedIn has more than 100 groups that can be useful for job seekers. Becoming part of the industry community where you want to work can give you an edge up.[15] Here are some typical Interest groups:

- Oil and Gas Jobs
- Jobs in the Shipping Industry
- Information Security Careers Network
- Mutual Fund and Investment Jobs and Careers
- Technology Jobs Network
- Public Relations and Communications Jobs Community
- Treasury/Finance Careers
- Green Jobs and Career Network
- Financial Services Career Network
- Event Planning and Event Management

There is even a Career Change Central site that links career changers with recruiters, a MyCredentials site for members to help each other with their resumes and interviews, a Job-Hunt Help (members sharing leads and advice), and a JobsDirectUSA, the official job search group in LinkedIn for JobsDirectUSA.com.[16]

Branding Yourself and Creating Greater Search Engine Optimization Reach

You need to get noticed. One way is to mount an organized campaign to be active and visible every day. An expert suggests you to plan on adding at least one "update" every day to share with your network. It can be a response to something you read that morning. By sharing it or liking it you can draw the attention of the person who wrote it. In addition, you can write and publish articles on LinkedIn.[17]

One general piece of advice is that you don't want to come across as constantly touting your own horn. So, follow the 532 rule. That means out of 10 postings, make sure 5 are curated posts about industry news, 3 original posts, and 2 personal/humanizing posts.[18] One expert suggests that you write articles on LinkedIn's blog which will negate your need to set up your own blog elsewhere.[19]

Using AI to Perform a LinkedIn Brand Audit

You can use generative AI to perform a personal brand audit of your presence. Tell it that its role is to act like a personal branding strategist. Its task is to analyze your current LinkedIn presence and identify any gaps or weaknesses. You paste in your Profile details. You can then ask it to rewrite your profile for maximum visibility and credibility so people will want to follow you.

Spotlight on a Career Changer

From Volunteering to a Life Coach

Liz Bell started by volunteering for a charity. Soon afterward she was hired as a volunteer manager. Unfortunately, she felt out of her depth and began to resent the tasks she was forced to do but felt were irrelevant. She complained and felt miserable. After taking a break from work for work-related stress. After some travel with her partner, she knew she wanted to work directly with people and help them achieve their goals. She became an English for Speakers of Other Languages (ESOL) teacher, but that was just a step on her path to becoming a life coach. She joined a group coaching program and began learning what it takes to build a coaching business. She passed the certification test and now has achieved her goal of becoming a life coach![20]

Cleaning Up Your Social Media

Remember that photo of you and your team celebrating a big client win with whiskey bottles all over the table—nice win but not a cool photo for your social media account. You want to be like the expression about Caesar's wife who almost must be "above reproach." So, if you wrote all kinds of emotional pieces on your blog or on Instagram after an election, scrub them because you never know what is going on in the mind of a potential recruiter. The same goes for any off-color jokes, pictures of wet T-shirt contests, complaints about your old company, or your membership in controversial groups as well as some of your attempts at self-promotion that in retrospect are way over the line.[21]

Beautifying Your Instagram Account

According to experts, your photo can be less formal than the one you post on LinkedIn. You need to be consistent in your Bio section to make sure your content is the same as it is on Facebook, X, and LinkedIn. Some people use hashtags in their bio. If people want more information about you, that's the place to put a link to your website. As in the case of all your social media, you need to clean up any pictures that convey the wrong image of you.[22]

Preparing Your X Account for Your Job Hunt

Even more than on other social media platforms, hashtags on X are important for visibility, and experts say it can improve your visibility by 33 percent on that platform. It is a place where you can carry on conversations with hiring managers. Experts also suggest you follow companies you are interested in so you can discuss the latest news they broadcast as well as the priorities they emphasize. Make sure you enable direction messaging with anyone as with your tweets which should be public.[23]

Using Facebook for Your Job Hunting

Facebook can be helpful for your job search. With your privacy settings set to private, you can tell your friends and family that you are looking for a position and ask for help. Experts suggest you make sure your public profile on Facebook contains keywords associated with your job search. You also can search Facebook for people by company or job title. If you find a person of interest who is connected to one of your friends, you can e-mail your friend to ask for an introduction. If a person of interest lists hobbies or volunteer interests, it gives you points of contact when you connect. Searching Facebook groups by city and the word "jobs" might reveal some leads. While Facebook's job board is not listed among the top job boards, it's worth taking a look.[24]

More Networking: Informational Interviews

Remember the searches we discussed earlier in the chapter that helped you locate people with the same job title you are seeking and, even, people who work at the same company? One of the networking tools that is catching on is the informational interview. Generally, 15 to 30 minutes over the phone or perhaps over coffee at a convenient location for the person being interviewed, this interview can give you real insights into the day-to-day activities of someone doing pretty much what you think you want to do. The result could be a new friend who can help you and even serve as a mentor. Or, equally important, it might reveal some dark side to the job that might make you rethink applying or, at least, applying to a particular company. The best way to get started is to write a polite e-mail. Spell out what you are doing now and why you would be interested in learning more about the person's job. Express gratitude for the time. There are all kinds of questions you can ask. You'll want to know about the life balance, the things the person likes the most and dislikes the most about the job, the company culture, and so on. Don't forget to ask if you can reconnect if you have any further questions and also if they might suggest someone else in the company you can talk with.[25]

Shadowing

Shadowing is also a form of social networking. You ask one of the people you've located as holding a job title and working at a company where you want to work whether or not you can shadow them for a short period of time. It gives you a chance to follow someone during their work day and get a real feel about the job. You also get a chance to network with the person you are shadowing, ask lots of questions, and meet other people at work who could become part of your network.[26]

Conclusion

Today social media and networking are critical tools for job hunters and, particularly for people changing careers. It is important to have a consistent appearance and send a consistent message on your various social media websites. LinkedIn contacts are critical as is growing the number of contacts because of the importance of second level and even third level contacts. The search ability of LinkedIn enables job seekers to find people within a desired company and even people with the same job title desired. This is critical for finding mentors as well as finding people you can shadow to learn more about the job and career path. Facebook has value because your friends and their friends might be able to deliver viable contacts to help you land an interview and job. Instagram and X are both critical because they make direct communicating with decision makers much easier and more natural.

CHAPTER 7

Mastering the Job Hunt

Brainstorming a New Career Using AI

AI tools can help you from the very beginning of a career change, the moment you begin brainstorming to find a possible new career, until the very moment you write your acceptance note. Let's start with brainstorming a possible new career. One young woman who is a writer began by feeding ChatGPT information on her goals, likes and dislikes. She also did not want to choose a career that had little prospects for growth so she also fed it a 290-page report from the World Economic Forum on the future of work. She also fed her AI her resume as well as what she liked and disliked about her job, information on certain industries that interested her, and instructed it to use everything it knew about her to identify lucrative career options.[1]

Just as working with a career coach requires iteration after iteration to fine tune career recommendations, generative AIs do as well. ChatGPT's first list consisted of writing-related jobs, so the woman had to indicate that she wanted a completely different career. Yet another iteration produced a job list the woman labeled as "too techy." When the woman added that she was interested in women's health and fertility, the agent came back with some suggestions that the woman found intriguing.

Another way to handle brainstorming a new career is to have your AI tool focus on transferable skills. You can ask your AI tool to examine your resume and identify your transferable skills and use that information to produce a list of 10 positions in different industries that you should qualify for.[2]

The AI Battle Between Employers and Candidates

There is a battle going on between employers' use of AI and applicants. The latest statistics indicate 99 percent of Fortune 500 companies use the Applicant Tracking System (ATS) to screen applicants' resumes based on correct formatting and presence of keywords. Those resumes with low

Spotlight on a Career Changer

From Finance Controller to Counselor

Suzanne Lluch spent 10 years in a small telecommunications company working her way up to Finance Controller. Miserable in her work, she took an "Introduction to Counselling" course at an adult learning center and decided that would be her goal, even though it would take several years to get there. She financed this career change by working as the Finance Director for a charity. Once she finished her education, she set up her private practice starting with just one day a week. She is now very happy.[3]

scores are eliminated before humans begin sorting through the top scoring resumes. Many services including Kickresume (kickresume.com) will score your resume and offer advice on how to raise its ATS score (https://www.kickresume.com/en/ats-resume-checker/) Pricing for Kickresume's service varies from monthly ($24), quarterly ($18/month) or annual ($8/month). The company has published some basic resume formatting rules applicants should follow.[4] These include:

- Using bullets instead of long paragraphs
- Bolding sections and job titles
- Using a single-column format
- Using a professional 10- to 12-point font such Times New Roman, Arial, or Calibri
- Using margins of 0.5 to 1 in
- One page if less than 10 years of experience, otherwise a full two pages
- Using the keywords found in the job description
- Submitting the resume in a PDF file format unless told to use a different format
- Including standard material such as contact information, education, work experience, summary or objective, and skills
- Line spacing of single to 1.15
- Consistency in date format for jobs listed

Using AI to Create Your Resume

If you are not comfortable using your own AI agents, you can subscribe to Jobscan (jobscan.co). It costs $29.98 on a quarterly basis or $49.95/month. Jobscan will scan your resume, provide you with an ATS score, and its AI will offer advice on optimizing your resume to match a particular job description. It uses AI to match your resume with jobs, cover letter generator, LinkedIn Optimizer, unlimited keyword comparisons and synonym detector, AI bullet point generator, ATS-friendly resume templates, a resume manager, and, of course, its job board.

Using Your AI to Generate an ATS-Friendly Resume

A number of services such as jobscan.com can provide you with resume templates. Once you have one you are comfortable with and one that achieves a high ATS score, you can use your ai to modify it for specific job descriptions. Specifically, you can ask it to generate a Qualifications section at the top of your resume based on a job description as well as specific guidance you give it such as the number of bullets describing your skills and experience matched to the job description as well as tasks you have performed that match the job requirements most closely. You also can ask it to extract key ATS terms from the job description, compare them with the words you use in your resume, and recommend changes where more ATS words can be inserted. Be sure to have it describe only relevant transferable skills and tell it not to display company names or dates. You even can have your ai provide a list for you of where you don't match up.

Since you are tailoring your resume and cover letter for each job, have your ai play a role as hiring manager for XYZ company. Tell it to review your resume for the particular job and then indicate the reasons you would reject me. Then ask it to rewrite those sections to make them stronger. You also can have your AI draft a cover letter. However, with all of the AI's efforts, be sure to monitor what it writes and modify it to sound like yourself and not like an AI.

The Standard Resume to Pass the ATS Test

ATS can't read fancy fonts, graphics, or other "fancy" additions to your resume, so keep it simple. One major issue is that the standard resume format is chronological in nature; that might not work if you are moving to a completely unrelated career where job titles are completely different and where you are relying on your transferable skills to sell yourself. In other situations, say you are moving to a related industry or have decided to stay in your same industry but boost your knowledge of AI, the chronological approach might be fine.

The Chronological Resume

Figure 7.1 shows a chronological resume for a candidate trying to make a lateral career change from a technical writing job to a technical writing job with an AI company. The candidate uses the CREDENTIALS section to show how he has enhanced his skill set in order to be able to write about AI.

The Career Changer Resume

Career changers do not fare well with a standard chronological resume because it usually does not highlight their strengths or give the applicant the opportunity to try to include key terms that the ATS is looking for. The answer is to modify the resume into a functional or hybrid format. Let's say Bill Jones has never had a job doing technical writing, but he wants to get a job in the technology field doing that kind of work. He needs a way to highlight his skills rather than his experience because his history of job titles will not match that of the traditional applicant. Figure 7.2 shows how a hybrid resume can help. It does offer some chronological job information to show that Bill has been steadily employed, but it starts with a functional skills approach. Remember how we've preached the importance of transferable skills. Here is a resume where those skills can be described.

BILL JONES

Mobil: 858-9999 Email: Billjones63@gmail.com

Technical writing professional with 7 years experience
Seeking a position with an AI company

EXPERIENCE

Techno Babble **Dec 2022-Present**
Senior Technical Writer
*Created, wrote, and edited company's monthly bulletin
*Wrote 15 software manuals
*Trained staff on how to write software manuals
*Developed method to save 20% of publishing costs

Software World **November 2020-Dec 2022**
Technical writer
Wrote news stories for a technical newsletter
Interviewed software engineers

Peptomine University **September 2017-June 2020**
Editor of PU Newspaper
Started as staff writer
Managed staff of 10 people
Edited all feature stories
Wrote monthly column

EDUCATION
Peptomine University **June 2020**
B.A. English with a minor in Computer Science

Skills
Time management, Interviewing, Attention to detail
Knowledge of Git, Markdown, JavaScript/Typescript, Python Jira, and GitLab/GitHub.
Experience using FrameMaker, Adobe Illustrator, Word

Certifications
Claude 101 (Anthropic)
AI Fluency: Framework & Foundations (Anthropic)
Building with Claude API (Anthropic)

Figure 7.1 **A chronological resume**

BILL JONES

Mobile: 858-9999 Email: Billjones63@gmail.com

Experienced writer with technology knowledge
Seeking position as a technical writer

Accomplishments and Skills

Writing & Editing Skills

- Researched and wrote department annual report for city agency
- Interviewed homeless & wrote City of Phoenix report on this topic
- Wrote articles for university newspaper

Technical Writing Software Expertise

- Knowledge of FrameMaker
- Knowledge of Microsoft Office
- Knowledge of Adobe Illustrator
- Certificate in Technical Writing

Knowledge of Technology

- Minor in Computer Science
- Knowledge of Macintosh and Windows computers

Skills
Time management, Interviewing, Attention to detail
Knowledge of Git, Markdown, JavaScript/Typescript, Python Jira, and GitLab/GitHub.
Experience using FrameMaker, Adobe Illustrator, Word

Professional Experience
Analyst, City of Phoenix **2020-2026**
Analyzed data & wrote reports for senior management

Salesman, Best Buy **2018-2020**
Explained complex hardware & software to customer
Hands-on experience with major software & hardware

Education
Pentomine University
B.A. English with a minor in Political Science

Figure 7.2 A hybrid resume for a career changer

The Major Job Boards

CareerBuilder (careerbuilder.com) offers a job search board as well as a resources section with information on different careers. Keep in mind that CareerBuilder and Monster have an agreement, so together they are stronger.

College Recruiter (collegerecruiter.com)—Geared to entry-level and internship jobs.

Hiring Café (hiring.cafe)—This website offers a good search engine where you can use Boolean operators to be specific including indicating what you do not want in your search. You also can hide your name and contact information until a company actually wants to talk with you. Hiring Café aggregates a huge number of other job boards. If you select nonprofit jobs, for example, you'll see jobs from at least 12 different very specialized job search sites.

Indeed (indeed.com)—Always listed among the best job boards. Indeed includes free skills tests and mock interviews. You also can browse companies and salaries for specific job titles as well as search with keywords and see other jobs offered by the same company.

LinkedIn (LinkedIn.com)—This job board is a must for job seekers and those planning on a career change. You can filter on jobs where you have contacts which is a nice feature. A couple of oft-mentioned complaints are that some companies post "ghost" jobs which don't really exist. Also, the sheer volume of applicants has some people convinced that if you don't set an alert and immediately apply within the first couple of days when a job is posted, your resume will be lost in the crowd or just ignored. See Chapter 6 for a lot more information on how to use LinkedIn effectively.

Monster (Monster.com) is another major job board. It also has a resume building tool as well as other resources including a salary calculator and information on various careers. One problem is that this website does not have the range of search filters other sites offer

Simply Hired (simplyhired.com)—Partners with Indeed so the same application process for both websites. Simply Hired aggregates jobs from a variety of sources. While tools are limited, it is possible to read reviews from people who work at a company where you are applying. The site does offer a salary estimator tool.

Zip Recruiter (ziprecruiter.com)—It has a large search engine. Its ai keeps job hunters appraised of their applications and also offers advice. Its "Seen First" feature allows a job hunter to "jump to the front of the line" by sending a short note along with the application.

Specialty Job Boards

A number of job boards specialize in particular industries and usually offer valuable information about the industries as well as companies in addition to job openings,

Dataaxy (Dataaxy.com)—Jobs in Data and AI. This site includes guides to resumes and interviews. It aggregates jobs from other sites like LinkedIn, Slack, and X

Dice (Dice.com)—Good for technical jobs but limited search capabilities

eFinancialCareers (efinancialcareers.com)—The website, at the time of writing, says you can search 68,739 jobs in finance and financial technology.

Government Jobs (governmentjobs.com)—Aggregates thousands of government jobs in one place.

Green Job Search (greenjobsearch.org)—Jobs in conservation, green energy, climate change, sustainability, and so on.

HR Crossing (HRcrossing.com)—This site focuses exclusively on human resource specialist jobs. It has a fee it says to weed out casual job "surfers." HR Crossing says it collects the most HR jobs, including those found on small overlooked job sites.

Idealist (idealist.com)—This website is ideal for nonprofit and volunteer jobs. It even includes internships. If your aptitude tests showed you had an interest in working for a company or organization that wanted to improve the world, this is your website to explore. It has resources on different types of nonprofit jobs and careers.

Mediabistro (mediabistro.com)—If your aptitude tests showed you were a "creative," this site is for you. It has a number of resources including online courses, as well as resume and coaching services. There is a job board focused on journalism, publishing, design, production, and marketing as well as other creative fields. The fee is 14.95/month.

National Council of Nonprofits Job Board (Councilofnonprofits.org)—The site offers the opportunity to browse hundreds of nonprofit jobs across the country.

Tech Careers (Techcareers.com)—It focuses exclusively on technology jobs.

Tech nonprofit Job Board by Fast Forward (jobs.ffwd.org)—Ideal for people with technical backgrounds who want to work for a nonprofit. The range is wide with jobs such as event planner, fundraiser, and software engineer for an immigration policy organization.

If none of these databases match your specific target, go to jobsearchdb.com. There you will find links to job databases covering 39 different industries including part-time work.

USA Jobs (usajobs.gov)—Lists government jobs as well as showing career paths.

The Cover Letter

While some companies have portals that only allow you to upload your resume, others might still permit a cover letter. This type of brief note can go a long way to differentiate your application because it can show your interest as well as spotlight your skills and say, in effect, "Be sure to look at my resume." Figure 7.3 offers a sample of a cover letter.

Conclusion

Generative AI can help when it comes to beating the application tracking system that many employers use. The key is to follow recommended formats and tweak your AI-generated resumes so they don't sound like they were written by an AI. Job hunters need to take advantage of the several specialized job boards available. A chronological resume is standard, but it might not be the best format for a resume written by a career changer. A hybrid resume enables the career changer to highlight transferable skills.

Figure 7.3 **A cover letter**

Your name
E-mail address
Phone Number

Date

Dear [Try to find the name of the hiring manager and use it if you can find it]

I am really interested and excited about the XYZ position with FIRM and the fact that FIRM does PHILANTHROPY [if mentioned on the website] or NEW PRODUCT or ANNOUNCEMENT. I would love to work with you on the XYZ project because it is such a close fit to my skills and interests.

Over X years I have demonstrated my ABC skills. In particular, my ability to [provide quantified evidence of your skills doing similar work. If you are a career changer, point to your transferrable skills]. Doing this work honed my XYZ skills.

I have an understanding of [Use key words from the job description] as well as a strong desire to exceed your highest expectations, and I would welcome the chance to work for you and for FIRM. I have attached a copy of my resume and would welcome the chance to talk with you about the POSITION and what skills and experience I can bring to FIRM.

Thanks so much for taking the time to read this note.

Regards

Your Name

CHAPTER 8

Preparing for Interviews as a Career Changer

Before the Interview

You've overcome the odds and received notice that you have an interview. Congratulations! Unfortunately, the bad news is that you have a lot of work to do before the interview. While you'll find information on the research you need to do prior to the meeting as well as the questions you need to practice in this chapter, some of your preparation involves making sure you will look as professional as possible. Make sure you have shoes shined, a recent haircut, and suit and shirts cleaned and pressed. It's a good idea to find out what the dress code is for the company. You can always over-dress and then remove your coat when you see people dressed more casually. You cannot go the other way. I used to do a lot of business travel (We're talking millions of air miles). My normal routine was to dress casually with jeans and tennis shoes and comfortably for the long flights but bring my suit and dress clothes in a separate bag. One day I was scheduled to meet with IBM back in the days when everyone there wore black suits, white shirts, and ties. I dressed that morning and discovered I had forgotten to pack my black dress shoes. What could I do?

I walked with a limp into the room to meet the IBM folks dressed in my suit, dress shirt, tie, and tennis shoes. When I saw several people staring at my shoes, I told them I had hurt my foot and needed to wear tennis shoes. I received a lot of sympathy as I sat down. Unfortunately, by the time the meeting was over I had forgotten which foot was "injured" so I could limp on that foot. Luckily no one noticed.

Using AI to Be Your Own Toughest Interviewer

I know one college senior who routinely gives his AI files containing the material he needs to know for a test and then instructs the AI to construct the hardest questions it can and then compare his answers with the correct answers. After doing this, his professor's questions seem easy. You will be doing something very similar to prepare for your interview.

Regardless of which generative AI you use, you'll want to follow a pattern. The University of Manchester's Careers Service suggests you Prepare, Prompt, and Proofread as a guide along with Role, Task, and Format. Preparation is providing your AI with the information it needs to help you. That means you want it to have your application, your resume, the company's description of the job you will interview for, and any other pertinent information you have on the company found on LinkedIn or other social media including its website. The prompting stage obviously is critical. First of all, you want to provide AI with the role it will be playing such as an experienced interview coach. You will be applying for the XYZ position at ABC company. You then list what tasks the AI needs to perform. Do you want it to ask interview questions about that specific job? How should it deliver the material? Do you want it to have you respond to each question and then assess your answer in terms of what the question is measuring and point out any deficiencies in your answer? Do you want it then to provide an answer from your resume and other materials that better answers the question? Finally, you should make sure the AI has all the material it needs about you, your job experience, transferable skills, volunteer experience, and so on.[1]

Another candidate might turn to its AI and tell it, "I'm interviewing for the XYZ position at ABC. Generate likely interview questions and evaluate my responses."Still a third might choose to ask an AI to generate behavioral questions such as "Tell me about yourself" and then evaluate his or her answers. Still another candidate might use this prompt: "In the role of my interview coach, based on the job description, generate 20 likely interview questions and answers using the STAR method (Situation, Task, Action, Result)."

Recent college graduates generally are very familiar with using generative AI, but if you've been out of school for a number of years it might only be something you've read about. So, what do you do if you want to use AI for your interview but don't have any experience using a generative AI or just don't feel comfortable because you only have superficial working knowledge? The answer is that there are countless companies that can help you for a fee.

Fee-Based AI Interview Tools

There are dozens of companies offering fee-based AI tools for mock interviews with assessment of your answers. Some even operate in stealth mode during your actual interview. Here is a list of some of the leading companies.[2]

Huru (Huru.ai) is not cheap ($24.99/month), but it does provide instant feedback on your mock interview answers and provides you with lots of questions.

Interview Ignitor (interviewignitor.com) is useful if you are considering technology occupations because it provides over 1,000 questions from real companies. It provides instant feedback on your answers. The pricing includes one-time fees varying from $9.99 to $39.99 depending on whether you want a one-week, one-month, or three-month subscription.

Final Round AI (finalroundai.com) not only provides mock interviews with feedback but can operate in stealth mode during your actual interview to help you answer questions based on your resume and whatever other information you have uploaded to it. It's expensive though, with prices based on a yearly ($41.67/month), quarterly ($99.67/month) or monthly ($149/month).

Lockedin AI (https://www.lockedinai.com) has a wide range of features including the ability to use Copilot to provide you (in stealth mode) with answers to interview questions in real time. The answers appear right on your screen but only you can see them. The website also has AI support for generating cover letters, resumes, optimizing your LinkedIn account, and career path advice. The cost for all this is high (US$54.99 monthly or US$39.99/month for three months). Tough Interview Question Simulator Prepares you for pressure moments. Prompt: Ask me 10 difficult interview questions commonly used by top companies (e.g. "Why should we not hire you?"). After each answer, critique it and suggest a high-performing response. There are additional tools available including the following:

Final Interview Readiness Test: Full Simulation

Prompt: Run a full 20-minute mock interview simulation for a [*Job Title*] role. Ask structured questions and evaluate me on the following areas: communication, problem solving, leadership, and cultural fit. End with a final hiring recommendation.

Company-Specific Prep Tailored Preparation for a Specific Employer

Prompt: I am interviewing at [*Company Name*] for a [*Job Title*] role. Generate:

- Likely interview questions
- What the company is really evaluating
- How I should position myself

Personal Pitch Creator (Tell Me About Yourself)

Craft a strong first impression.

Prompt: Create a 60-second professional answer for "Tell me about yourself" based on this background: [*Paste background*]

AI Interview Masters

AI Interview Masters (aiinterviewmasters.com) is a website that includes mock interviews, a quiz builder, and (with the premium model) deep analytics and analysis of your responses and up to 20 mock interviews a month. This service charges $9/month with premium services for $24/month. The premium pricing includes GPT 5.

Interview Prep AI (interviewprep-ai.com)

The program is very intuitive. The AI asks the questions orally and in writing and understands oral responses. It provides an analysis of strengths and weaknesses of answers at the end of the interview.

Pricing is: free for one interview, €10 for up to 5 interviews, and €19.2 for up to 12 interviews.

Researching the Interviewer

"To whom will I be speaking?" That's the very first step toward researching the one who during that one hour will be the most important person in your life. What you want to discover, of course, are any points of contact, similar interests, hobbies, volunteer work, specific work accomplishments, and so on. One place to start is to see if any of your LinkedIn contacts are connected to your interviewer. You also should pour over any material about this person on the company's website.

Your search has just begun. The next stage is to use Google. Don't stop there, though. Google is not the only search engine with its own crawler and AI, so be sure to try a few others. Start with Microsoft's Bing and use its AI Copilot to see if you can find any additional information. Other search engines worth using are Perplexity (Perplexity.ai), DuckDuckGo (duckduckgo.com), ChatGPT's search capability (https://chatgpt.com), and Brave (search.brave.com). If the company is public, see if you can access some yearly reports.

Don't neglect social media. You can look at your interviewer's LinkedIn page although you won't be able to see his or her contacts since you're not connected. What about his X.ai (Twitter) account? Does he have a Facebook page or an Instagram page?

Research the Company and Prepare Questions

The same search engines that you used to find information about your interviewer can also provide information about the company. In addition, if the company is public you will want to read the usually very illuminating quarterly reports when the CEO talks with Wall Street financial analysts. Here you'll learn about new products and new directions for the company. Of course, you also will want to read the press releases and sections where they usually are links to articles about the company on the company's website. Keep in mind how you could play a part in any new directions or product lines the company is pursuing. It also provides you with an opportunity when asked if you have any questions to work this information you learned into your questions as well as to do so earlier in the interviewer should the opportunity arise.

As an example, it is not unusual for an interviewer to ask you why you want to work for this specific company. Obviously, you're not going to say that you need a job and you saw this opening. Imagine, though, if you could answer that you are very excited about the company developing an XYZ product or moving into the ABC market and you would love to be able to work on these products. I have mined lots of gold in the company's quarterly report transcripts over the years. Similarly, if a company issues stock, you need to read the Initial Public Offering (IPO) prospectus carefully since it will, by law, need to lay out the major competitors and risks the company faces as well as its opportunities. You also can turn to your 401k provider such as Schwab or Fidelity to use their online research services to find out what the company's financial report card looks like. Your interviewer will be very impressed with your knowledge of the company as an outsider.

The Day of the Interview

Do give yourself lots of time to drive to your interview. Arrive early enough to get comfortable, use the restroom if required, and do a last-minute visual check as well as calm your nerves. Bring a copy of your resume and cover letter so you can refer to them or answer questions about them. Be sure to greet the receptionist cordially and introduce yourself. Once I worked for a manager who would solicit his receptionist's input on how candidates treated her because he didn't want to hire someone who treated people badly if they didn't feel they needed to impress them.

Types of interviews

AI Agents

Who would have guessed a few years ago that the first round of some interviews today would be conducted by an AI agent? You are more likely to have one of these interviews if you're in a technical field because the agent tends to ask specific questions about your skills and skill levels. If you just review what you listed on your resume and respond with answers about the classes or certificates you hold, this should just be a small step until the next step in the interview process.

The Telephone Interview

The telephone interview could be conducted with an AI agent or with someone from HR. After all, it's simply a screening interview. There are some tips to keep in mind. You want to be upbeat and smile. Yes, even though it's not a video call, your smile comes across in a telephone conversation. You also want to make sure you are not interrupted during the call.

A Word About Video Interviews

Most of us have had at least one technology disaster with Zoom during the COVID-19 period. The lesson to be learned is that you need to do everything you can to minimize the possibility of a technology disaster. What that means starts with your computer and Internet connection. Make sure you've closed all the programs you don't need to run the video software. Make sure you've blocked all alerts. If other people in your family share your Internet connection, have them agree to not be on your wireless connection during the interview. If a certain browser is recommended, then use it even if it is not your favorite. If the company has a way for you to test the connection ahead of time, do so. We'll talk about facing the camera and other ways of coming across well on a video call shortly.

The Prerecorded Video or One-Way Video Interview

This is a relatively new type of interview. You'll be provided with some questions to read or some short videos to watch, and then you will be asked to record your responses via video.

Experts warn not to read ahead because often you will not be able to return to the current question. Some software allows you to have multiple tries to answer the questions while others do not.[3] VidCruiter interviews generally consist of five to six prerecorded competency-based ("Describe your knowledge of C++ programming") or behavioral questions ("Tell us about yourself" or "What are your weaknesses?") with a 30-second preparation timer and a two-minute recording limit per answer. You should have a stop-watch or your phone handy to make sure you are not cut off mid-sentence. It is a good idea besides practicing answering these types of questions to have material in bullet form that you can look at during the preparation period.

The Live Video interview

As in the case of the prerecorded video interview, you will want to control the physical and technical environment as much as possible. Remember, realtors "stage" houses in order to help them sell better. Be sure to silence your various devices and make sure that your e-mail and other alerts are set to not display during the interview. A few years back I watched a video interview with Josh Shapiro, the then attorney general of Pennsylvania. During the interview his teenage son walked into the room and right past Shapiro, presumably unaware that a live video interview was taking place. To avoid such interruptions, be sure you have alerted everyone to not enter your office during the interview. If you don't have a home office and have to use another room in the house, make it look as businesslike as possible.

Your backdrop is a reflection of you and your values, so you want to eliminate any clutter and maybe place objects there that convey the image you want to project. Are you applying for a managerial position, if so, then you might want to display a few books on leadership along with any awards you've earned. Technically, it is critical that you adjust the lighting so you don't look like a criminal being interrogated under too bright a light. Similarly, lighting that is too low is distracting for the interviewer. Wearing headphones will help eliminate the possibility of any echoing. Of course, as in the case of any interview, you'll dress as if you were being interviewed in person. Positioning yourself in front of your computer camera is critical. You'll want your head and shoulders centered. You'll also want to focus on looking directly at the camera and not at the screen.[4] It's not a bad idea to hold a dress rehearsal, perhaps over Zoom with a friend, to test how you are coming across before the actual interview.[5]

Group Interviews

I've had group interviews although they tend to be more common if you're applying for a job with a government agency or university. The idea of a group interview is that everyone gets to ask certain questions that are the same questions asked of every candidate. They then score your answers. The idea is that it provides HR with a way of pointing out just how honest the interview process is. All candidates received the same treatment. It also eliminates the need for trained interviewers since the questions are decided ahead of time. One of the challenges in this type of interview is for you to focus on the interviewer while also providing some eye contact with the other interviewers when you answer questions. Often the questions will involve providing you with a situation and asking how you would respond. See the discussion in this chapter on behavioral interviews and the link in that section to the most common questions and good answers to those questions if you'd like to practice answering such questions. When the interviewers introduce themselves, take note what their job functions are. If someone is from Operations and another person is from Finance, you will want to answer your questions but also add anything that relates to those departmental functions and establish eye contact when you do so.

I have to say that group interviews can be distracting because you're dealing with three or more people who all have different body language signals they are sending. I had one such interview where one person kept taking a loud chomp of an apple whenever I started to respond to a question. It probably wouldn't fly today, but I went to one group interview scheduled for 4 p.m., right after work. I figured everyone's blood sugar would be very low and they might find it hard to concentrate so I brought homemade cookies and passed them out. Nowadays who knows if someone might react by thinking I was trying to poison the panel? In my case, the cookies were a big hit and I did get that job.

The Future Colleague Interview

I've had plenty of this type of interview. Generally, if you are a finalist, you'll often be asked to not only meet with the decision maker but also to have a separate interview with one or more of the people who would be your colleagues should you be hired. They're primary concern is whether or not they would enjoy working with you and, psychologically, whether or not you're someone they would like to go out for lunch with. Try to get a sense from their questions where they are coming from. One future colleague asked three questions about my background and then switched to talking about San Diego Charger football. A few years later when I actually became his boss I asked him about this strange interview. His answer was that he decided I knew my stuff and he was fine with working with me so he decided to talk about his favorite topic and see if I shared his interest. Obviously, in a team environment you can understand why you probably will field questions on how well you work in a team environment, so you might want to come to the interview with some examples in hand.

The Unstructured Interview

The unstructured interview is also known as the nondirective interview. The interviewer begins with an open-ended question and then uses the interviewee's answers as springboards to additional questions. So, for example, an interviewer might begin by saying, "Tell me about yourself" or "Do you remember an occasion when you were faced with XYZ?"[6] These unstructured questions can seem overwhelming without a system with which to respond. A career coach with 20 years' experience in career advising recommends using a Past, Present, and Future model. In other words, you could respond to an unstructured question by describing what you accomplished or did in the past, what you currently are doing, and your goals or plans moving forward. He provides another example. If the interviewer asks you how you handled a specific problem, you could respond how you handled a similar problem in the past, how you would use your problem-solving skills today to solve that problem, and how you hope to keep refining those skills to solve similar problems in the future.[7]

In order to feel more comfortable and to enable you to practice answering unstructured interview questions, Resume Genius has listed the 35+ most common behavioral interview questions. The five most common behavioral interview questions include "Tell me about how you worked effectively under pressure" and "Can you give me an example of a time when your team member disagreed with you."[8] Tatum Hunter offers her own list of 35 behavioral interview questions but adds how to answer them.[9]

What to Do with a Bad Interviewer

Sometimes you will be stuck with someone who is a bad interviewer. In some cases, it might be because he had to hurry from one meeting to another meeting and had no time to prepare, but more likely he is someone who is not used to conducting interviews but was thrown in as a last-minute replacement. This situation happened to me. I found myself taking over the interview and saying, "Let me tell you about myself," and later, "There are a number of reasons why I would like to work here." I even asked him, "What do you like best about working here?" and then chiming in how much those reasons resonated with my reasons for joining the company. The point is that you should have an agenda. There are certain things you need to get across to an interviewer, especially your journey that brought you to the point of changing careers and also why you specifically want to work at XYZ company. Your job is to get those points across.

Handling the Career Change Question

The key, of course, is to make your career change seem like the most natural move you could make. For one job interview I had carefully analyzed all the tasks that the new position would require and then made a list of what I did with my transferable skills to show that I already was doing the job. Another job required a switch to a completely different industry. I came armed with statistics and reasons why I was so excited about the future for that industry and for that company since its CEO had announced a couple of new initiatives in one of his quarterly financial meetings with Wall Street analysts. Your career change might be the result of a particular project you worked on (This was true for one of my career changes) or a part of your current or past job that you really enjoyed even though it represented only a small portion of your total job. The point is to paint a story that makes sense. Once again, this is a situation where you could ask your AI to help you: "As a job recruiter analyze my resume and the job description of the job I am seeking and come up with reasons why this new job represents a logical career change."

The Salary Question

The old saying used to be that the one who brought up the salary first loses. That's not necessarily true, but you don't want to kill your chances by coming across as inflexible. If you have to answer the question, provide a range based on Glassdoor.com's "Know Your Worth" tool.[10] You can switch the focus when asked what your salary expectations are by asking what is the budgeted range for this position? It is also possible to say that your salary is negotiable based on learning more about your role and your team, your benefits, and the rest of the package, but you would expect a salary somewhere in the range of A to B. You can also point out that according to Glassdoor the position in the particular city where the company is generally has a range of X to Y.

Sometimes this question will come up as a screening question on one of the first interviews you have with the company. If so, try to avoid a direct answer by saying you need to learn more about the position and your role before coming up with a firm number. The salary is negotiable depending on a lot of factors that haven't come up yet, such as your role, your opportunities for advancement, and your benefits.

Spotlight on a Career Changer

Elizabeth Draper: Filmmaker to Gluten-Free Baker

Elizabeth was on a career path that led her to marketing and distribution jobs with several independent film companies. At the age of 48 she lost her job. What direction should she go? Since her two big loves were film making and baking, she decided to try baking. She began by baking and then trying to sell her goods at street markets. Often the key to success is finding a way to meet the decision maker. In this case, Elizabeth heard about a new café opening and camped out until she could talk with the decision makers to sell them her gluten-free cakes. It took her eight months to convince them, but she finally succeeded. During the interim she continued to sell her cakes at street markets. Now the company buys her cakes for their other branches. One regret Elizabeth shares with other career changers is that she regrets she didn't make her career shift five years earlier.[11]

Beginning, Performing, and Concluding the Interview Well

Smile and greet your interviewer with a firm but not bone crushing handshake and maintain eye contact. One way I prepared for the interview to make sure I was relaxed and comfortable and exuded confidence is to use the visualization technique Michael Jordan and other successful athletes have used to achieve extraordinary performances. Spend time preparing for the interview by imagining the interview and how successful you will be during that interview. Imagine how you will feel as you answer questions smoothly and confidently. Imagine how pleased you will be when the interviewer asks you questions you already have prepared for.

During the interview ask questions to clarify any questions that raise questions in your mind. Make the interview interactive so you can learn about the company while the interviewer is learning about you. Respond to interviews by describing a problem you faced, how you dealt with it, and what results you achieved.

The Most Common Questions You Likely Will Face

The best way to prepare for these types of questions is to practice saying them aloud. I used to practice in front of a mirror. Here is a list of some of the more common questions you might face:

Questions to Show How Well You Know Yourself

Tell me about yourself.
You should have a short answer down pat before the interview. Be able to describe your career arc and why you are so interested in this particular job and company. What have you learned about yourself that led you to want to apply for this job, particularly if it represents a career change?

What motivates or drives you?
Here's the time to talk about your desire to be successful and to do what makes you happy.

What are your strengths and weaknesses?
You do not want to follow the now discredited advice to try to make a strength a weakness. Don't try the "I'm just too concerned about achieving the company's goals routine." Instead, describe a weakness you have recognized and have worked on. As far as strengths, pick out a couple of them; if you can point to actual statements by other team members or your ex-boss, you can use those: "I was told by my boss

that he's never known me to miss a deadline" or "I had a salesperson tell me that he always wants me to go with him on his sales calls because I help close the deals." As far as weaknesses, pick one that you have since worked on such as a difficulty in accepting help or a difficulty in handling criticism. The point is to show how well you know yourself.

How do you handle stress?

Companies want to see if you have approved ways of handling stress. Do you take yoga? Do you swim after work? Do you run? Pretty much any answer works except binge drinking or binge eating.

How would your coworkers describe you?

Focus on how you helped them and the team solve problems and move ahead. Would they call you creative, (Can you think of an example?) well-organized, a hard worker, and so on?

What accomplishment are you most proud of?

Once again, you should be ready for this question by relying on the STAR approach to describe the situation that represented a challenge for you, what actions you took, and what the results were. If you can quantify this answer, more the better: "We had an attrition rate of 20 percent that was costing us a fortune to refill these positions. I did XYZ, and the results were a X percent increase in retention."

Tell me about a difficult decision you had to make.

You should be able to use the STAR approach to describe a situation, the task, the difficulty you faced, the actions you took, and the results. Have a number of these stories ready in case you need them in the interview.

Tell me about a time you failed and what you learned.

Once again, it's good to have a story ready, including in retrospect why you failed and what you learned from the experience. Be honest and don't try to turn a negative into a positive (i.e.; "I tried too hard").

Tell me about a time you faced an ethical dilemma? How did you handle it?

It might be a situation where you were tempted to cut corners to meet a deadline or a time you noticed an employee breaking a rule or, perhaps, a time a colleague or team member wanted the group to do something you felt wasn't right. Have a story to cover this question in your back pocket just in case.

Resume Questions

There appears to be a gap in your resume. How do you explain this?
Naturally there is a gap because you may have been laid off. Perhaps you have a gap between you had to help a sick spouse or child or relocate for a family reason. Explain this gap in terms of what you've done to make good use of your time before your next job and/or new career move. Did you decide that you wanted to take the time to learn enough about AI so that you could use it to work more efficiently? Did you use the time to fill a different gap in your background?

Your resume says you have a "working knowledge" of XYZ. What do you me by that?
Particularly for any technical skills you've listed on your resume, you can expect a question or two on some of those skills.

I notice you have jumped from job to job. How do I know you won't do that with this position?
Nobody wants to get a reputation as a job hunter, but sometimes circumstances demand it. Don't bad-mouth your previous managers, but point out limitations you saw that couldn't be addressed when it came to opportunities for growth.

Interpersonal Skills Questions

Tell me how you dealt with a disagreement between you and another team member.
The interviewer wants to see how well you work with other members of a team, particularly when you are not in a managerial position. Think about a situation where you did have a disagreement and then describe how you used your persuasive skills or negotiating skills to understand the root cause of the person's disagreement, how you addressed his concerns, and how you solved the problem.

Tell me about a time you disagreed with your boss?
This is a variant of the previous question but this time you are dealing with your supervisor or manager who has power over you. The way to answer the question is to point to how you presented your case and tried to persuade your boss but went along with his or her decision on the matter. In other words, you were a good soldier.

Questions About the Company

Why do you want to work for our company?
Here's where all your research on the company comes into play. Are you excited about their new products? If so, why? Is the company high on the list of best companies to work for? Have you been following trends and see how the company is moving into an area earlier than its competitors and you want to be part of that? Remember not only to read the company's annual reports, but also transcripts of the CEO's quarterly meetings with financial analysts. You just need a few nuggets to impress the interviewer that you've done your homework.

Questions to See if You Fit into the Company Culture

Are you willing to work nights and weekends to meet a deadline?
Eager beaver that you are, you don't want to come across as a workaholic who will burn out, but you do want to come across as a team player who will do what is necessary for the team to succeed. Have a story ready where your team was under tremendous time restraints and still met the deadline.

Are you willing to relocate?
If you are, let them know. If not, be honest.

What are your long-term objectives? How do you see yourself in three years?
The interviewer is really asking how long before you jump to another company? The old stock answer of saying you want your manager's job in three years is NOT the way to answer the question. You want to stress how you want to improve various skills and abilities so that you can be someone other members of the team turn to when they need answers.

Questions to Ask at the End of the Interview

As far as the conclusion of your interview, your interviewer is likely to ask you if you have any questions. No is not a good answer. Of course you have questions! Your research should have turned up a number of questions about the company, and here is your chance to ask them. In addition, here are some useful questions to ask:

Who will be my manager and what is his title?
You want to find out the title of the person managing you to get a handle on how the team is organized.

What happened to the last person to hold this position?
If he were promoted, that's a good sign. If he quit, that does raise some red flags.

What do you see as the most important tasks I will be expected to perform?
Having them prioritize your responsibilities gives you information you can use in pointing out your strengths and experience in some of these areas when you summarize why you want the position.

Do you offer employees opportunities for professional growth and development?
The point is to show that you want to keep improving your skills and abilities.

When will I hear from you?
You need to have a realistic expectation when you'll receive word about the next step.

After the Interview

Thought you were finished with the process? Think again. You still need to write a follow-up letter.

The Follow-Up Letter

Waiting for a follow-up call or note after your interview can be very painful. Be sure to follow up immediately after your interview. You enjoyed meeting with the interviewer, you are particularly excited about the prospect of you using your skills that align so well with the company's needs to work on ABC. Remind the interviewer about how they said your knowledge of XYZ or experience doing ABC would be particularly valuable in your role. You are looking forward to hearing from the interviewer and you mention that he or she should feel free to contact you should they have any additional questions. Of course, you hope to hear from them soon.

Conclusion

Your generative AI can help you prepare by generating interview questions from the job description and company website. You must be prepared for a variety of interviews that include use of an AI bot, one-way interviews, telephone interviews, video interviews, structured and unstructured interviews, and group interviews. You can use your generative AI to help research the individual who will be interviewing you. It is important to study the company website, news releases, and even tweets to be able to ask questions about the company to the interviewer. Be sure to write a letter of thanks after the interview since it is one more chance to "touch" the interviewer and remind him or her of your interest.

Endnotes

Preface

1. Stan Schatt and Michele Lobl, *Paint Your Career Green: Get a Green Job Without Starting Over* (JIST Works, 2012).
2. Schatt and Lobl, *Paint Your Career Green.*

Chapter 1

1. CBS News, "What are the Prospects for Laid-off Workers?" December 14, 2025, accessed February 10, 2026, https://www.cbsnews.com/news/this-week-on-sunday-morning-dec-14-2025/.
2. Jeannine Mancini, "IBM Plans to Replace Nearly 8,000 Jobs with AI—These Jobs are First to Go," *YahooFinance.com*, May 5, 2023, accessed February 26, 2026, https://finance.yahoo.com/news/ibm-plans-replace-nearly-8-174052360.html.
3. Preston Fore, "Microsoft Researchers Have Revealed the 40 Jobs Most Exposed to AI—And Even Teachers Make the List," January 29, 2026, accessed February 26, 2026, https://fortune.com/article/what-are-the-jobs-most-exposed-to-ai-microsoft-research/.
4. Fore, "Microsoft Researchers."
5. Nexford Team, "How Artificial Intelligence Will Change the World," *Nexford University*, January 15, 2026, accessed February 26, 2026, https://www.nexford.edu/insights/how-will-ai-affect-jobs.
6. John Koetsier, "Report: Jobs That Are Most and Least Impacted By AI," *Forbes*, February 25, 2026, accessed March 27, 2026, https://www.forbes.com/sites/johnkoetsier/2026/02/25/report-jobs-that-are-most-and-least-impacted-by-ai/.
7. Jordan Valinksy, "Amazon Is Laying Off 16,000 Employees as AI Battle Intensifies," January 28, 2026, accessed February 26, 2026, https://www.cnn.com/2026/01/28/tech/amazon-layoffs-ai.
8. Dallas Gagnon, "Layoffs Surge in 2026: 10 Major Companies Slashing Thousands of Jobs," February 24, 2026, accessed March 8, 2026, https://www.masslive.com/news/2026/02/layoffs-surge-in-2026-10-major-companies-slashing-thousands-of-jobs.html.
9. Natallie Rocha, "Block Cuts 40% of Work Force Because of Embrace of A.I.," *New York Times*, February 26, 2026, https://www.nytimes.com/2026/02/26/technology/block-square-job-cuts-ai.html?smid=nytcore-ios-share.

10. Michael Feroli, "Is AI Already Impacting Job Growth?" August 15, 2025, accessed February 26, 2026, https://www.jpmorgan.com/insights/global-research/artificial-intelligence/ai-impact-job-growth.
11. Ian D. Wyatt and Daniel E. Hecker, "Occupational Changes During the 20th Century," *Monthly Labor Review, Bureau of Labor Statistics*, 2006, accessed February 26, 2026, https://www.bls.gov/opub/mlr/2006/03/art-3full.pdf.
12. James Manyika, James, Susan Lund, Michael Chui, et al., "Jobs Lost, Jobs Gained: What the Future of Work Will Mean for Jobs, Skills, and Wages," *McKinsey & Company*, November 28, 2017, accessed February 26, 2026, https://www.mckinsey.com/featured-insights/future-of-work/jobs-lost-jobs-gained-what-the-future-of-work-will-mean-for-jobs-skills-and-wages.
13. Thomas H. Davenport and Laks Srinivasan, "Companies Are Laying Off Workers Because of AI's Potential—Not Its Performance," *Harvard Business Review*, January 29, 2026, accessed March 2, 2026, https://hbr.org/2026/01/companies-are-laying-off-workers-because-of-ais-potential-not-its-performance
14. Ben Johnson, "The Great Horse Manure Crisis of 1894," accessed February 26, 2026, https://www.historic-uk.com/HistoryUK/HistoryofBritain/Great-Horse-Manure-Crisis-of-1894/.
15. Fiona Jack, "I Felt a Constant Sense of Imposter Syndrome," accessed March 17, 2026, https://www.careershifters.org/success-stories/from-education-to-animal-welfare.
16. Anderson Cooper and Nichole Marks, "Why Anthropic CEO Dario Amodei Spends So Much Time Warning of AI's Potential Dangers," November 16, 2025, accessed February 27, 2026, https://www.cbsnews.com/news/anthropic-ceo-dario-amodei-warning-of-ai-potential-dangers-60-minutes-transcript/.
17. HIGH5 Content Team & Review Team, "Comprehensive Career Change Statistics in the US," April 23, 2025, accessed February 26, 2026, https://high5test.com/career-change-statistics/.
18. Ray A. Smith, "The Number of Americans Wanting to Switch Jobs Hits a 10-Year High," *Wall Street Journal*, December 3, 2024, accessed February 26, 2026, https://www.wsj.com/lifestyle/careers/job-satisfaction-low-gallup-data-detachment-17bc183c.
19. Caroline Castrillion, "Why 50% of Americans Think It's Time for a Career Change," *Forbes*, April 22, 2025, accessed February 23, 2025, https://www.forbes.com/sites/carolinecastrillon/2025/04/09/why-50-of-americans-think-its-time-for-a-career-change/.

Chapter 2

1. Alex Reed, "5 Signs It's Time for a Career Pivot," February 4, 2026, accessed February 28, 2026, https://vault.com/blogs/changing-jobs/5-signs-it-s-time-for-a-career-pivot.
2. Heidi Borst, "Starting a New Career in My 40s was the Hardest and Most Rewarding Thing I've Ever Done," May 2, 2024, accessed March 17, 2026, https://www.businessinsider.com/career-change-forties-rewarding-hard-2024-5.

Chapter 3

1. David Kyle, "AI is Now Mandatory: The New Performance Review," *LinkedIn*, May 2026, accessed July 8, 2026, https://www.linkedin.com/posts/kyle-david_ai-is-now-mandatory-the-new-performance-activity-7449758898409848832-K9ZL/.
2. Vlada Korzun, "Best AI Tools for Teachers 2026: Lesson Plans, Grading & Safety," *Coursiv*, March 13, 2026, https://coursiv.io/blog/best-ai-tools-for-teachers-2026.
3. Matthew Haag, "In N.Y.C. Classes, Teachers Can Use A.I. to Plan but Not to Assign Grades," *New York Times*, March 24, 2026, accessed March 24, 2026, https://www.nytimes.com/2026/03/24/nyregion/ai-nyc-classes-grades.html?smid=nytcore-ios-share.
4. Marnal BNS, "How AI Saved My Career (and Took It to the Next Level)," *Medium*, September 11, 2024, accessed March 24, 2026, https://medium.com/@MissManal.Bns/how-ai-saved-my-career-and-took-it-to-the-next-level-6f2d594c75af.
5. Indeed Editorial Team, "Making a Lateral Career Move: A Complete Guide, December 11, 2025, accessed March 23, 2026, https://www.indeed.com/career-advice/career-development/lateral-career-move; please also see Leslie Stevens-Huffman, "Smart Career Moves for People in Tech Jobs Facing Disruption from AI," February 28 2024, accessed March 23, 2026, https://www.dice.com/career-advice/smart-career-moves-for-tech-jobs-facing-disruption-from-ai.
6. Jennifer Inglis, "The 5 Most Valuable Generative AI Certifications," accessed March 23, 2026, https://www.coursereport.com/blog/the-5-most-valuable-generative-ai-certificates.
7. Inglis, "The Five Most Valuable AI Certifications."
8. John McGoldrick, "Top 10 Highest Paying Artificial Intelligence Jobs & Salaries 2026," *Nexford University*, January 25, 2026, accessed March 23, 2026, https://www.nexford.edu/insights/highest-paying-ai-jobs.

Chapter 4

1. "O*NET® Interest Profiler Manual," March 2021, https://www.onetcenter.org/reports/IP_Manual.html.
2. The Myers-Briggs Company, "Developing Self-Awareness to Unlock Potential," https://www.themyersbriggs.com/en-US/Explore-Solutions/MBTI.
3. MBTI, "Find Your Ideal Career," https://www.mbtionline.com/en-US/Products/For-your-career.
4. Career Assessment Site, "The Strong Interest Inventory® Test," https://career-assessmentsite.com/tests/strong-tests/about-the-strong-interest-inventory/.
5. Ash Ayvar De Alcaraz, "The CAPBOI Personality Model: A Game-Changer in Your Career Path Selection," November 21, 2023, accessed February 23, 2026, https://www.jobtest.org/learn/capboi-model.
6. Joshua Nelken-Zitser, "I Quit my Job, Went Back to School, and Started a New Career in My 40s. I Learned 3 Lessons About Starting Again," February 21, 2026, accessed April 1, 2026, https://www.businessinsider.com/quit-job-back-school-new-career-masters-40s-start-again-2026-2.
7. MIT Career Advising and Professional Development, "Using the STAR Method for Your Next Behavioral Interview (Worksheet Included)," accessed February 23, 2026, https://capd.mit.edu/resources/the-star-method-for-behavioral-interviews/.
8. Jeff Weber, "'Soft' Is an Understatement: The Importance of Transferable Skills," *Forbes*, April 26, 2019, accessed February 23, 2026, https://www.forbes.com/councils/forbeshumanresourcescouncil/2019/04/26/soft-is-an-understatement-the-importance-of-transferable-skills/.
9. Kai Strickland, "Transferable Skills Guide: Identifying Your Transferable Skills," *Addgene*, January 11, 2018, accessed February 23, 2026, https://blog.addgene.org/transferable-skills-guide-identifying-your-transferable-skills.

Chapter 5

1. John Koetsier, "Report: Jobs that are Most and Least Impacted by AI," *Forbes*, February 25, 2026, accessed March 27, 2026, https://www.forbes.com/sites/johnkoetsier/2026/02/25/report-jobs-that-are-most-and-least-impacted-by-ai/.
2. Nare Khachatryan, "The 10 Careers AI Won't Replace: Future-Proof Careers for the AI Era," March 15, 2026, accessed March 26, 2026, https://prometai.app/blog/10-jobs-ai-wont-replace-future-proof-careers-for-the-ai-era.
3. Amy Livingston, "20 Great Career Fields for the Future (Next 10 Years)," July 21, 2023, accessed March 27, 2026, https://www.moneycrashers.com/great-career-fields-for-the-future/.

4. Hank Pellissier, "40 Up-and-Coming Careers that Don't Require a 4-year College Degree (and 9 to Avoid), July 18, 2025, accessed March 29, 2026, https://www.greatschools.org/gk/parenting/college-and-career/great-careers-without-college-degree/.
5. Emily Gertenbach, "120 Jobs That AI Won't Replace," November 10, 2025, accessed March 27, 2026, https://www.upwork.com/resources/jobs-ai-wont-replace.
6. Jessica Stillman, "21 Future Jobs the Robots Are Actually Creating," December 6, 2017, accessed March 27, 2026, https://www.inc.com/jessica-stillman/21-future-jobs-robots-are-actually-creating.html.
7. U.S. Career Institute, "Top 65 Jobs Safest from AI & Robot Automation," February 2023, accessed March 28, 2026 https://www.uscareerinstitute.edu/blog/65-jobs-with-the-lowest-risk-of automation-by-ai-and-robots.
8. Dave Chaffey, "15 Applications of Artificial Intelligence in Marketing," February 14, 2024, accessed March 29, 2026, https://www.smartinsights.com/managing-digital-marketing/marketing-innovation/15-applications-artificial-intelligence-marketing/.
9. Tracy Brower, "50 Top Jobs to Consider When Making a Career Change," *Forbes*, March 12, 2024, accessed March 28, 2026, https://www.forbes.com/sites/tracybrower/2024/03/12/best-jobs-to-consider-when-making-a-career-change/.
10. Harriet Hoult, "I Got to a Point Where My Heart Wasn't in It Anymore. I'd Lost All My Energy and Motivation," accessed March 29, 2026, https://www.careershifters.org/success-stories/from-advertising-to-art.
11. Bureau of Labor Statistics, U.S. Department of Labor, Occupational Outlook Handbook, "Heating, Air Conditioning, and Refrigeration Mechanics and Installers," August 28, 2025, accessed March 26, 2026, https://www.bls.gov/ooh/installation-maintenance-and-repair/heating-air-conditioning-and-refrigeration-mechanics-and-installers.htm.
12. O*NET OnLine, "Welders, Cutters, Solderers, and Brazers," accessed March 29, 2026, https://www.onetonline.org/link/summary/51-4121.00.

Chapter 6

1. Ed Han, "10 Parts of an Effective LinkedIn Profile," accessed March 30, 2026, https://www.job-hunt.org/effective-linkedin-profile/.
2. Jenny Foss, "4 Key Elements of a Stellar Linked in Summary," *The Muse*, September 8, 2021, accessed March 30, 2026, https://www.themuse.com/advice/4-key-elements-of-a-killer-linkedin-summary.
3. Lily Zhang, "3 Smart Ways to Attract Recruiters to Your LinkedIn Profile," *The Muse*, September 18, 2020, accessed March 30, 2026, https://www.themuse.com/advice/3-smart-ways-to-attract-recruiters-to-your-linkedin-profile.

4. Muse Editors, "The 32 Best LinkedIn Profile Tips Every Professional Should Know," *The Muse*, November 29, 2024, accessed March 31, 2026, https://www.themuse.com/advice/the-31-best-linkedin-profile-tips-for-job-seekers.
5. Muse Editors, "The 32 Best LinkedIn Profile."
6. Gregory Austin, "How to Search Someone's Connections & Find People on LinkedIn," linkedin.com, August 19, 2019, accessed March 30 2026, https://www.linkedin.com/pulse/how-search-someones-connections-find-people-linkedin-austin-/.
7. Austin, "How to Search Someone's Connections."
8. Sara Hildebrand, "Setting Job Alerts on Linked In," accessed March 31, 2026, https://cooper.edu/continuing-education/setting-job-alerts-linkedin.
9. Sophie Ricci, "LinkedIn InMail Vs. Email: Which One Wins for Sales & Marketing in 2025?" October 7, 2025, accessed March 31, 2026, https://salesso.com/blog/linkedin-inmail-vs-email/.
10. Hunter, https://hunter.io/email-finder.
11. Ricci, "LinkedIn InMail Vs. Email."
12. Hunter, https://hunter.io/email-finder.
13. Ricci, "LinkedIn InMail Vs. Email."
14. Jonathan Perry, "Using Company Search," *LinkedIn*, February 11, 2021, accessed March 31, 2026, https://www.linkedin.com/pulse/linkedin-secrets-identifying-companies-using-company-search-perry/.
15. Tana Storani, "Top 100 Useful LinkedIn Groups for Job Seekers and Recruiters," *LinkedIn*, July 23, 2021, accessed March 30, 2026, https://www.linkedin.com/pulse/top-100-useful-linkedin-groups-job-seekers-recruiters-tana-storani/.
16. Chris Perry, "Top 25 LinkedIn Job Seeker Groups: To Help Build Your Brand and Launch Your Career," accessed March 30, 2026, https://career-potential.com/career-advice-article/top-25-linkedin-job-seeker-groups.
17. Susan P. Joyce, "5 Essential Elements of an Effective LinkedIn Presence," accessed March 31, 2026, https://www.job-hunt.org/linkedin-job-search-basics/.
18. Zhang, "3 Smart Ways to Attract Recruiters to Your LinkedIn Profile."
19. Meg Guioeppi, "Guide to Personal Branding with LinkedIn," accessed March 31, 2026, https://www.job-hunt.org/linkedin-personal-branding/.
20. Liz Bell, "My Career Change Story," *LinkedIn*, January 31, 2023, accessed March 31, 2026, https://www.linkedin.com/pulse/my-career-change-story-liz-bell-finding-your-happy/.
21. Phyllo. "20 Types of Red Flag Behavior Found on Social Media Background Checks," January 21, 2026, accessed March 30, 2026, https://www.getphyllo.com/post/20-red-flag-behavior-found-on-social-media-background-checks.
22. Hannah Morgan "How to Get Your Instagram Profile Ready for Your Job Search," accessed March 31, 2026, https://www.job-hunt.org/instagram-job-search-guide/.

23. The Interview Guys, "How to Use X to Get a Job: The 2026 Guide to Landing Roles on Twitter's Successor," June 25, 2026, accessed July 3, 2026, 2026, https://blog.theinterviewguys.com/how-to-use-x-to-get-a-job/
24. Hannah Morgan, "Guide to Facebook for Job Search Success," accessed June 30, 2026, https://www.job-hunt.org/facebook-job-search-guide/.
25. Jenny Foss, "How to Ask for (& Make the Most of) an Informational Interview," *LinkedIn*, August 30, 2022, accessed March 31, 2026, https://www.linkedin.com/pulse/how-ask-make-most-informational-interview-jenny-foss/.
26. Muse Editors, "Job Shadowing: Is It Any Good? Here's What to Consider," *The Muse*, October 31, 2024, accessed March 31, 2025, https://www.themuse.com/advice/job-shadowing.

Chapter 7

1. Amanda Smith, "I Used ChatGPT to Plan a Career Pivot and Found It Empowering," June 10, 2025, accessed March 6, 2026, https://www.cnet.com/tech/services-and-software/i-used-chatgpt-to-plan-a-career-pivot-and-found-it-empowering/.
2. LinkedIn Learning Blog, "How to Use AI to Help with Your Job Search," September 30, 2024, accessed March 6, 2026, https://www.linkedin.com/business/learning/blog/job-seeking-tips/ai-powered-job-searching-strategies.
3. Suzanne Lluch, "I was Utterly Miserable in My Job," accessed March 29, 2026, https://www.careershifters.org/success-stories/from-finance-to-counselling.
4. Klara Cervenanska, "How to Format a Resume? This Is the Best Resume Format for 2026 (+ Resume Examples)," January 13, 2026, accessed March 9, 2026, https://www.kickresume.com/en/help-center/how-to-format-resume/.

Chapter 8

1. University of Manchester Careers Service, "Your Guide to Using AI for Interview Preparation," accessed March 3, 2026, https://www.careers.manchester.ac.uk/applicationsinterviews/interviews/aiinterviewprep/.
2. Saptak Chaudhuri, "Best AI Tools for Interview Preparation," August 4, 2025, accessed March 3, 2026, https://geekflare.com/best/ai-powered-interview-preparation-platforms/.
3. Lauren Barber, "How to Ace Your Video Interview," Vidcruiter.com, June 23, 2025, accessed March 2, 2026, https://vidcruiter.com/video-interviewing/how-to-ace-your-interview/.

4. Ronda Suder, "10 Tips to Help You Ace Your Next Virtual Interview," October 28, 2024, accessed March 2, 2026, https://topresume.com/career-advice/10-tips-to-help-you-ace-your-next-virtual-interview.
5. James Hu, "Zoom Interviews: 8 Tips for Your Video Interview," *Jobscan blog*, November 14, 2024, accessed March 2, 2026, https://www.jobscan.co/blog/zoom-interviews-8-tips-for-your-video-interview/.
6. Delve, "Unstructured Interviews," accessed March 29, 2026, https://delvetool.com/blog/unstructured.
7. Neil James, "Mastering Unstructured Interview Questions with Past, Present, and Future Model," November 5, 2024, accessed March 2, 2026, https://bselected.com/mastering-unstructured-interview-questions-with-the-past-present-and-future-model/.
8. Conrad Benz, "35+ Most Common Behavioral Interview Questions," October 30, 2024, accessed March 2, 2026, https://resumegenius.com/blog/interview/behavioral-interview-questions.
9. Tatum Hunter, "35 Behavioral Interview Questions and How to Answer Them," September 9, 2025, accessed March 2, 2025, https://builtin.com/articles/behavioral-interview-questions.
10. Glass House Team, "How to Negotiate Your Salary," March 16, 2023, accessed March 6, 2026, https://www.glassdoor.com/blog/guide/how-to-negotiate-your-salary/.
11. Lucia Knight, "Martine Robins—International HR Director of Local HR Franchise Owner," October 5, 2017, accessed March 17, 2026, https://www.midlifeunstuck.com/jam-makers-1/2017/10/5/martine-roberts-international-hr-director-to-local-hr-franchise-owner.

Bibliography

Adam, Jamela. "Best Job Search Sites." May 30, 2025. Accessed March 11, 2026. https://careers.usnews.com/advice/outside-voices-careers/articles/best-job-search-sites.

Apt Team. "Best Job Boards in 2025: Top Alternatives to LinkedIn for Finding Your Dream Job." Accessed March 11, 2026. https://www.tryapt.ai/blog/best-job-boards-alternatives-to-linkedin.

Austin, Gregory. "How to Search Someone's Connections & Find People on LinkedIn." *LinkedIn,* August 19, 2019. Accessed March 30 2026. https://www.linkedin.com/pulse/how-search-someones-connections-find-people-linkedin-austin-/.

Barber, Lauren. "How to Ace Your Video Interview." June 23, 2025. Accessed March 2, 2026. https://vidcruiter.com/video-interviewing/how-to-ace-your-interview/.

Bell, Liz. "My Career Change Story." *LinkedIn,* January 31, 2023. Accessed March 31, 2026. https://www.linkedin.com/pulse/my-career-change-story-liz-bell-finding-your-happy/.

Benz, Conrad. "35+ Most Common Behavioral Interview Questions." October 30, 2024. Accessed March 2, 2026. https://resumegenius.com/blog/interview/behavioral-interview-questions.

BNS, Marnal. "How AI Saved My Career (and Took It to the Next Level)." *Medium,* September 11, 2024. Accessed March 24, 2026. https://medium.com/@MissManal.Bns/how-ai-saved-my-career-and-took-it-to-the-next-level-6f2d594c75af.

Boogaard, Kat. "The 17 Best Niche Job Search Websites to Help You Cut Through All the Clutter." *The Muse*. March 14, 2025. Accessed March 11, 2026. https://www.themuse.com/advice/the-17-best-niche-job-search-websites-to-help-you-cut-through-all-the-clutter.

Borst, Heidi. "Starting a New Career in My 40s Was the Hardest and Most Rewarding Thing I've Ever Done." May 2, 2024. Accessed March 17, 2026. https://www.businessinsider.com/career-change-forties-rewarding-hard-2024-5.

Brophy, Hailey. "The 6 Best Job Search Sites Ranked." *Resume-now.com,* January 21, 2026. Accessed March 11, 2026. https://shorturl.at/I03Sc.

Brower, Tracy. "50 Top Jobs to Consider When Making A Career Change." *Forbes,* March 12, 2024. Accessed March 28, 2026. https://www.forbes.com/sites/tracybrower/2024/03/12/best-jobs-to-consider-when-making-a-career-change/.

Bureau of Labor Statistics, U.S. Department of Labor, Occupational Outlook Handbook. "Heating, Air Conditioning, and Refrigeration Mechanics and

Installers." August 28, 2025. Accessed March 26, 2026. https://www.bls.gov/ooh/installation-maintenance-and-repair/heating-air-conditioning-and-refrigeration-mechanics-and-installers.htm.

Castrillion, Caroline. "Why 50% of Americans Think It's Time for a Career Change." *Forbes*, April 22, 2025. Accessed February 23, 2025. https://www.forbes.com/sites/carolinecastrillon/2025/04/09/why-50-of-americans-think-its-time-for-a-career-change/.

CBS News. "What are the Prospects for Laid-off Workers? December 14, 2025. Accessed February 10, 2026. https://www.cbsnews.com/news/this-week-on-sunday-morning-dec-14-2025/.

Cervenanska, Klara. "How to Format a Resume? This Is the Best Resume Format for 2026 (+ Resume Examples)." January 13, 2026. Accessed March 9, 2026. https://www.kickresume.com/en/help-center/how-to-format-resume/.

Chaffey, Dave. "15 Applications of Artificial Intelligence in Marketing." February 14, 2024. Accessed March 29, 2026. https://www.smartinsights.com/managing-digital-marketing/marketing-innovation/15-applications-artificial-intelligence-marketing/.

Chaudhuri, Saptak. "Best AI Tools for Interview Preparation." August 4, 2025. Accessed March 3, 2026. https://geekflare.com/best/ai-powered-interview-preparation-platforms/.

Chen, Lauren, and Luke Burgar. "How Do You Apply to Jobs in the Age of AI?" *The Panther*, February 19, 2026. Accessed March 3, 2026. https://www.thepanthernewspaper.org/news/how-do-you-apply-to-jobs-in-the-age-of-ai.

Cooper, Anderson, and Nichole Marks. "Why Anthropic CEO Dario Amodei Spends So Much Time Warning of AI's Potential Dangers." November 16, 2025. Accessed February 27, 2026. https://www.cbsnews.com/news/anthropic-ceo-dario-amodei-warning-of-ai-potential-dangers-60-minutes-transcript/.

Craig, Susan. "6 Tips for Using Social Media to Grow Your Career." April 21, 2022. Accessed March 30, 2026. https://vault.com/blogs/career-readiness/how-to-use-social-media-to-grow-your-career.

Davenport, Thomas H., and Laks Srinivasan. "Companies Are Laying Off Workers Because of AI's Potential—Not Its Performance." *Harvard Business Review*, January 29, 2026. Accessed March 2, 2026. https://hbr.org/2026/01/companies-are-laying-off-workers-because-of-ais-potential-not-its-performance.

De Alcaraz, Ash Ayvar. "The CAPBOI Personality Model: A Game-Changer in Your Career Path Selection." November 21, 2023. Accessed February 23, 2026. https://www.jobtest.org/learn/capboi-model.

Delve. "Unstructured Interviews." Accessed March 29, 2026. https://delvetool.com/blog/unstructured.

Eddleblute, Shireen, and Joshua Nelken-Zitser. "I Gave Up a C-Level Career in Investments to Write Children's Books. I Wanted to Build Something That

Could Outlive Me." *Business Insider*, August 26, 2025. Accessed March 8 2026. https://www.businessinsider.com/left-investment-c-suite-role-write-kids-books-about-money-2025-8.

Feroli, Michael. "Is AI Already Impacting Job Growth?" August 15, 2025. Accessed February 26, 2026. https://www.jpmorgan.com/insights/global-research/artificial-intelligence/ai-impact-job-growth.

Fore, Preston. "Microsoft Researchers Have Revealed the 40 Jobs Most Exposed to AI—And Even Teachers Make the List." January 29, 2026. Accessed February 26, 2026. https://fortune.com/article/what-are-the-jobs-most-exposed-to-ai-microsoft-research/.

Foss, Jenny. "4 Key Elements of a Stellar Linked in Summary." *The Muse*. September 8, 2021. Accessed March 30, 2026. https://www.themuse.com/advice/4-key-elements of a killer-linkedin-summary.

Foss, Jenny. "How to Ask for (& Make the Most of) an Informational Interview." *LinkedIn*, August 30, 2022. Accessed March 31, 2026. https://www.linkedin.com/pulse/how-ask-make-most-informational-interview-jenny-foss/.

Gagnon, Dallas. "Layoffs Surge in 2026: 10 Major Companies Slashing Thousands of Jobs." February 24, 2026. Accessed March 8, 2026. https://www.masslive.com/news/2026/02/layoffs-surge-in-2026-10-major-companies-slashing-thousands-of-jobs.html.

Gertenbach, Emily. "120 Jobs That AI Won't Replace." November 10, 2025. Accessed March 27, 2026. https://www.upwork.com/resources/jobs-ai-wont-replace.

Glass House Team. "How to Negotiate Your Salary." March 16, 2023. Accessed March 6, 2026. https://www.glassdoor.com/blog/guide/how-to-negotiate-your-salary/.

Grady, Kayte. "11 Best Job Search Apps for 2026." Accessed March 11, 2026. https://www.tealhq.com/post/best-job-search-apps.

Greenwald, Erin. "45 Things to Do on Social Media to Find Jobs." *The Muse*. January 31, 2025. Accessed March 30, 2026. https://www.themuse.com/advice/45-things-to-do-on-social-media-to-find-jobs.

Guioeppi, Meg. "Guide to Personal Branding with LinkedIn." Accessed March 31, 2026. https://www.job-hunt.org/linkedin-personal-branding/.

Haag, Matthew. "In N.Y.C. Classes, Teachers Can Use A.I. to Plan But Not to Assign Grades." *New York Times*, March 24, 2026. Accessed March 24, 2026. https://www.nytimes.com/2026/03/24/nyregion/ai-nyc-classes-grades.html?smid=nytcore-ios-share.

Han, Ed. "10 Parts of an Effective LinkedIn Profile." Accessed March 30, 2026. https://www.job-hunt.org/effective-linkedin-profile/.

Hann, Katherine. "8 Best Free Job Posting Sites of 2025." *Forbes*, September 12, 2025. Accessed March 11, 2026. https://www.forbes.com/advisor/business/best-free-job-posting-sites/.

Herbert, Marsha. "How to Use AI to Prepare for a Job Interview." *TopResume.com*, October 29, 2023. Accessed March 3, 2026. https://topresume.com/career-advice/how-to-use-ai-to-prepare-for-a-job-interview.

High 5 Content Team & Review Team. "Comprehensive Career Change Statistics in the US." April 23, 2025. Accessed February 26, 2026. https://high5test.com/career-change-statistics/.

Hildebrand, Sara. "Setting Job Alerts on Linked In." Accessed March 31, 2026. https://cooper.edu/continuing-education/setting-job-alerts-linkedin.

Hoover, Amanda. "RIP Resumes." *Business Insider*, March 3, 2026. Accessed March 10, 2026. https://www.recruitingnewsnetwork.com/posts/rip-resumes.

Hoult, Harriet. "I Got to a Point Where My Heart Wasn't in It Anymore. I'd Lost All My Energy and Motivation." Accessed March 29, 2026. https://www.careershifters.org/success-stories/from-advertising-to-art.

Hu, James. "Zoom Interviews: 8 Tips for Your Video Interview." *Jobscan blog*, November 14, 2024. Accessed March 2, 2026. https://www.jobscan.co/blog/zoom-interviews-8-tips-for-your-video-interview/.

Hunter, Tatum. "35 Behavioral Interview Questions and How to Answer Them." September 9, 2025. Accessed March 2, 2025. https://builtin.com/articles/behavioral-interview-questions.

Indeed Editorial Team. "Making a Lateral Career Move: A Complete Guide." December 11, 2025. Accessed March 23, 2026. https://www.indeed.com/career-advice/career-development/lateral-career-move.

Inglis Jennifer. "The 5 Most Valuable Generative AI Certificates." Accessed March 23, 2026. https://www.coursereport.com/blog/the-5-most-valuable-generative-ai-certificates.

Jack, Fiona. "I Felt a Constant Sense of Imposter Syndrome." Accessed March 17, 2026. https://www.careershifters.org/success-stories/from-education-to-animal-welfare.

James, Neil. "Mastering Unstructured Interview Questions with Past, Present, and Future Model." November 5, 2024. Accessed March 2, 2026. https://bselected.com/mastering-unstructured-interview-questions-with-the-past-present-and-future-model/.

Johnson, Ben. "The Great Horse Manure Crisis of 1894.". Accessed February 26, 2026. https://www.historic-uk.com/HistoryUK/HistoryofBritain/Great-Horse-Manure-Crisis-of-1894/.

Joyce, Susan P. "5 Essential Elements of an Effective LinkedIn Presence." Accessed March 31, 2026. https://www.job-hunt.org/linkedin-job-search-basics/.

Khachatryan, Nare. "The 10 Careers AI Won't Replace: Future-Proof Careers for the AI Era." March 15, 2026. Accessed March 26, 2026. https://prometai.app/blog/10-jobs-ai-wont-replace-future-proof-careers-for-the-ai-era.

Knight, Lucia. "Martine Robins—International HR Director of Local HR Franchise Owner." October 5, 2017. Accessed March 17, 2026. https://www.midlifeunstuck.com/jam-makers-1/2017/10/5/martine-roberts-international-hr-director-to-local-hr-franchise-owner.

Knight, Lucia. "Elizabeth Draper—Film Business Executive to Gluten-free Baker." April 5, 2024. Accessed March 8, 2026. https://www.midlifeunstuck.com/jam-makers-1/2018/4/24/elizabeth-draper-film-business-executive-to-gluten-free-baker.

Koetsier, John. "Report: Jobs That Are Most and Least Impacted By AI." *Forbes*, February 25, 2026. Accessed March 27, 2026. https://www.forbes.com/sites/johnkoetsier/2026/02/25/report-jobs-that-are-most-and-least-impacted-by-ai/.

LearnHowtoBecome.org Staff. "Learn How to Become's 15 Best Job Search Sites." May 1, 2023. Accessed March 30, 2026. https://www.learnhowtobecome.org/career-resource-center/15-best-job-search-sites/.

LinkedIn Learning Blog. "How to Use AI to Help with Your Job Search." September 30, 2024. Accessed March 6, 2026. https://www.linkedin.com/business/learning/blog/job-seeking-tips/ai-powered-job-searching-strategies.

Livingston, Amy. "20 Great Career Fields for the Future (Next 10 Years)." *Money Crashers*, July 21, 2023. Accessed March 27, 2026. https://www.moneycrashers.com/great-career-fields-for-the-future/.

Lluch, Suzanne. "I Was Utterly Miserable in My Job." Accessed March 29, 2026. https://www.careershifters.org/success-stories/from-finance-to-counselling.

Mancini, Jeannine. "IBM Plans to Replace Nearly 8,000 Jobs with AI—These Jobs are First to Go." *YahooFinance.com*, May 5, 2023. Accessed February 26, 2026. https://finance.yahoo.com/news/ibm-plans-replace-nearly-8-174052360.html.

Manyika, James, Susan Lund, Michael Chui, et al. "Jobs Lost, Jobs Gained: What the Future of Work Will Mean for Jobs, Skills, and Wages." *McKinsey & Company*, November 28, 2017. Accessed February 26, 2026. https://www.mckinsey.com/featured-insights/future-of-work/jobs-lost-jobs-gained-what-the-future-of-work-will-mean-for-jobs-skills-and-wages.

McGoldrick, John. "Top 10 Highest Paying Artificial Intelligence Jobs & Salaries 2026." *Nexford University*, January 25, 2026. Accessed March 23, 2026. https://www.nexford.edu/insights/highest-paying-ai-jobs.

MIT Career Advising and Professional Development. "Using the STAR Method for Your Next Behavioral Interview (Worksheet Included)." Accessed February 23, 2026. https://capd.mit.edu/resources/the-star-method-for-behavioral-interviews/.

Morgan, Hannah. "How to Get Your Instagram Profile Ready for Your Job Search." Accessed March 31, 2026. https://www.job-hunt.org/instagram-job-search-guide/.

Muse Editors. "Job Shadowing: Is It Any Good? Here's What to Consider." *The Muse*. October 31, 2024. Accessed March 31, 2025. https://www.themuse.com/advice/job-shadowing.

Muse Editors. "The 32 Best LinkedIn Profile Tips Every Professional Should Know." *The Muse*. November 29, 2024. Accessed March 31, 2026. https://www.themuse.com/advice/the-31-best-linkedin-profile-tips-for-job-seekers.

Nelken-Zitser, Joshua. "I Quit my Job, Went Back to School, and Started a New Career in My 40s. I Learned 3 Lessons About Starting Again." February 21, 2026. Accessed April 1, 2026. https://www.businessinsider.com/quit-job-back-school-new-career-masters-40s-start-again-2026-2.

Nexford Team. "How Artificial Intelligence Will Change the World." *Nexford University*, January 15, 2026. Accessed February 26, 2026. https://www.nexford.edu/insights/how-will-ai-affect-jobs.

O*NET OnLine. "Welders, Cutters, Solderers, and Brazers." Accessed March 29, 2026. https://www.onetonline.org/link/summary/51-4121.00.

Pellissier, Hank. "40 Up-and-Coming Careers That Don't Require a 4-Year College Degree (and 9 to Avoid)." July 18, 2025. Accessed March 29, 2026. https://www.greatschools.org/gk/parenting/college-and-career/great-careers-without-college-degree/.

Perry, Chris. "Top 25 LinkedIn Job Seeker Groups: To Help Build Your Brand and Launch Your Career." Accessed March 30, 2026. https://careerpotential.com/career-advice-article/top-25-linkedin-job-seeker-groups.

Perry, Jonathan. "LinkedIn Secrets: Identifying Companies Using Company Search." *LinkedIn*, February 11, 2021. Accessed March 31, 2026. https://www.linkedin.com/pulse/linkedin-secrets-identifying-companies-using-company-search-perry/.

Peters, Paul. "Best Job Boards for 2025." January 8, 2025. Accessed March 11, 2026. https://www.betterteam.com/job-boards.

Phyllo. "20 Types of Red Flag Behavior Found on Social Media Background Checks." January 21, 2026. Accessed March 30, 2026. https://www.getphyllo.com/post/20-red-flag-behavior-found-on-social-media-background-checks.

Reed, Alex. "5 Signs It's Time for a Career Pivot." February 4, 2026. Accessed February 28, 2026. https://vault.com/blogs/changing-jobs/5-signs-it-s-time-for-a-career-pivot.

Ricci, Sophie. "How to Get Contact Info from LinkedIn Without Connection." Accessed March 31, 2026. https://salesso.com/blog/to-get-contact-info-from-linkedin-without-connection/.

Ricci, Sophie. "LinkedIn InMail Vs. Email: Which One Wins for Sales & Marketing in 2025?" October 7, 2025. Accessed March 31, 2026. https://salesso.com/blog/linkedin-inmail-vs-email/.

Rocha, Natallie. "Block Cuts 40% of Work Force Because of Embrace of A.I." *New York Times*, February 26, 2026. https://www.nytimes.com/2026/02/26/technology/block-square-job-cuts-ai.html?smid=nytcore-ios-share.

Schatt, Stan. *Still Room for Humans: Career Planning in an AI World.* Business Expert Press, 2023.

Schatt, Stan, and Michele Lobl. *Paint Your Career Green: Get a Green Job Without Starting Over.* JIST Works, 2012.

Segal, Noam. "How to Use AI for Your Next Job Interview." *Lenny's Newsletter*, February 24, 2026. Accessed March 8, 2026. https://www.lennysnewsletter.com/p/how-to-use-ai-in-your-next-job-interview.

Setup. "3 Awesome (Free) Tools Every Job Seeker Should Use." Accessed March 31, 2026. https://setup.us/blog/3-awesome-free-tools-every-job-seeker-should-use.

Smith, Amanda. "I Used ChatGPT to Plan a Career Pivot and Found It Empowering." June 10, 2025. Accessed March 6, 2026. https://www.cnet.com/tech/services-and-software/i-used-chatgpt-to-plan-a-career-pivot-and-found-it-empowering/.

Smith, Ray A. "The Number of Americans Wanting to Switch Jobs Hits a 10-Year High." *Wall Street Journal*, December 3, 2024. Accessed February 26, 2026. https://www.wsj.com/lifestyle/careers/job-satisfaction-low-gallup-data-detachment-17bc183c.

Stevens-Huffman, Leslie. "Smart Career Moves for People in Tech Jobs Facing Disruption from AI." February 28, 2024. Accessed March 23, 2026. https://www.dice.com/career-advice/smart-career-moves-for-tech-jobs-facing-disruption-from-ai.

Stillman, Jessica. "21 Future Jobs the Robots Are Actually Creating." December 6, 2017. Accessed March 27, 2026. https://www.inc.com/jessica-stillman/21-future-jobs-robots-are-actually-creating.html.

Storani, Tana. "Top 100 Useful LinkedIn Groups for Job Seekers and Recruiters." *Linkedin*, July 23, 2021. Accessed March 30, 2026. https://www.linkedin.com/pulse/top-100-useful-linkedin-groups-job-seekers-recruiters-tana-storani/.

Strickland, Kai. "Transferable Skills Guide: Identifying Your Transferable Skills." *Addgene*, January 11, 2018. Accessed February 23, 2026. https://blog.addgene.org/transferable-skills-guide-identifying-your-transferable-skills.

Suder, Ronda. "10 Tips to Help You Ace Your Next Virtual Interview." October 28, 2024. Accessed March 2, 2026. https://topresume.com/career-advice/10-tips-to-help-you-ace-your-next-virtual-interview.

The Interview Guys. "How to Use X to Get a Job: The 2025 Guide to Landing Roles on Twitter's Successor." June 25, 2026. Accessed July 3, 2026. https://blog.theinterviewguys.com/how-to-use-x-to-get-a-job/.

University of Manchester Careers Service. "Your Guide to Using AI for Interview Preparation." Accessed March 3, 2026. https://www.careers.manchester.ac.uk/applicationsinterviews/interviews/aiinterviewprep/.

U.S. Bureau of Labor Statistics. "Number of Jobs, Labor Market Experience, Marital Status, and Health for Those Born 1957–1964." August 26, 2025. Accessed March 6, 2026. https://www.bls.gov/news.release/pdf/nlsoy.pdf.

U.S. Career Institute. "Top 65 Jobs Safest from AI & Robot Automation." February, 2023. Accessed March 28, 2026 https://www.uscareerinstitute.edu/blog/65-jobs-with-the-lowest-risk-of-automation-by-ai-and-robots.

Valinsky, Jordan. "Amazon Is Laying Off 16,000 Employees as AI Battle Intensifies." January 28, 2026. Accessed February 26, 2026. https://www.cnn.com/2026/01/28/tech/amazon-layoffs-ai.

Weber, Jeff. "'Soft' Is an Understatement: The Importance of Transferable Skills." *Forbes*, April 26, 2019. Accessed February 23, 2026. https://www.forbes.com/councils/forbeshumanresourcescouncil/2019/04/26/soft-is-an-understatement-the-importance-of-transferable-skills/.

Whitfield, Brennan. "Is Your Job AI-Proof? What to Know About AI Taking Over Jobs." *Built In*, January 8, 2026. Accessed March 8, 2026. https://builtin.com/artificial-intelligence/ai-replacing-jobs-creating-jobs.

Wyatt, Ian D., and Daniel E. Hecker. "Occupational Changes During the 20th Century." *Monthly Labor Review, Bureau of Labor Statistics*, 2006. Accessed February 26, 2026. https://www.bls.gov/opub/mlr/2006/03/art3full.pdf.

Zhang, Lily. "3 Smart Ways to Attract Recruiters to Your LinkedIn Profile." *The Muse*. September 18, 2020. Accessed March 30, 2026. https://www.themuse.com/advice/3-smart-ways-to-attract-recruiters-to-your-linkedin-profile.

Appendix

Table A.1 Certificate programs by providers

Note: Keep in mind that classes are listed alphabetically so that classes in industries such as wine making, project management, and digital analytics might be listed differently, so be sure to read through the entire listing. Once you have identified some programs you like, look up the specific institutions to determine their cost, the number of classes required for a certificate, and so on.

Title of Credential	Abbrev
A+ & Security + Certification Prep	SM
Account-Based Marketing Bootcamp	HUBS
Note: HUBS offers a series of very short online classes (a few hours each) that do provide certificates. They do not offer formal university certificates but they are useful for filling in specific gaps in someone's background such as knowledge of specific software.	
Accounting	IndTec
Accounting	MASS
Accounting	SNU
Accounting	BISM
Accounting	SB
Accounting (grad)	PENNS
Accounting (grad)	PURD
Accounting and Finance	UPAC
Accounting Data Analytics (grad certificate)	Illinois
Accounting Foundations	MARY
Accounting Foundations (grad)	PENNS
Accounting Foundations (grad certificate)	Illinois
Accounting Fundamentals	WGU
Accounting Information Security (grad)	MARY
Acquisition & Contract Management (grad)	MARY
ACT Complete Life Coaching Certificate Adv to Exp	UDEMY

(continued)

Table A.1 Certificate programs by providers (continued)

Title of Credential	Abbrev
Note: Life coaching is a growing field. While a few universities offer credentials, this program is more comprehensive since it offers certificates for different levels of expertise.	
Adaptive Healthcare Strategy	CORN
Addiction and Recovery (grad)	UF
Additive Manufacturing	IndTec
Additive Manufacturing & Design (grad)	PENNS
Administrative Professional	UPAC
Adobe Certificated Professional in Visual Design	UPAC
Adobe Content Creator	Coursera
Note: One of the easiest ways to enhance a job in digital design is to fill in gaps in your knowledge of specific (and often very difficult) software.	
Advanced Digital and Social Media (grad certificate)	TexasT
Advanced Analytics (graduate certificate)	Illinois
Advanced Certificate in Biomedical Quality Systems	SDSU
Advanced Certificate in Digital Assets and Services	SJ
Advanced Certificate in Public Health	SDSU
Advanced Certificate in Regulatory Affairs	SDSU
Advanced Certificate in Web & Mobile Applications Dvp	SDSU
Advanced Conference and Wedding Management (grad certificate)	TexasT
Note: There are several listings in this Appendix for certificate programs for both wedding planners and event planners. These are excellent people-oriented careers that AI is not likely to replace.	
Advanced Counter-terrorism & Homeland Security (grad certificate)	SNU
Advanced Creative Operations Silver	RUT
Advanced Cybersecurity (grad)	PHOE
Advanced Entrepreneurship (grad certificate)	TexasT
Advanced Entrepreneurship in the Services Industry	TexasT
Advanced Forensic DNA Technology (grad)	UF
Advanced Google Analytics (Google)	CLASS
Advanced Hospitality Revenue Management: Pricing & Demand	CORN
Advanced Legal Research and Writing	UPAC
Advanced Management	MARY
Advanced Manufacturing (grad)	UF
Advanced Paralegal	UPAC
Advanced Paralegal Certificate	LB
Advanced Product Management	STANF

Title of Credential	Abbrev
Advanced Program Project Management	UDEMY
Advanced Safety and Health	DH
Advanced Software Developer (grad)	PHOE
Advanced Teaching Strategies for Agriculture Education (grad)	Illinois
Advanced Wastewater Collection Systems	RUT
Advancing K-12 STEM Master Teacher Leadership (graduate)	TexasT
Advertising & Marketing	REG
Aerodynamics & Flight Mechanics (graduate certificate)	Illinois
Aerospace Structural Mechanics (graduate certificate)	Illinois
Agentic AI Architecture	CORN
Agentic AI (Johns Hopkins)	GRT
Agentic AI for Beginners	UDEMY
Agribusiness (graduate certificate)	TexasT
Agricultural Biosecurity & Food Defense (grad)	PENNS
Agricultural Communications Leadership (graduate certificate)	TexasT
Agricultural Leadership (graduate certificate)	TexasT
Aha! Product Management Professional	LINK
AI & Machine Learning Bootcamp	LSU
AI + Civil and Environmental Engineering (graduate certificate)	Illinois
AI and Business Innovation	IndTec
AI and ML: Leading Business Growth (MIT)	GRT
AI Automation	LSU
AI Business Strategy (Johns Hopkins)	GRT
AI Engineering (grad)	PENNS
AI For Everyone	BOISE
AI for HR Professionals	LSU
AI for Marketing	LSU
AI for Marketing, Sales & Service Bootcamp	HUBS
Note: There are several courses in this Appendix that provide credentials in the use of AI in a specific discipline such as Marketing, HR, and Agriculture. They are ideal for those seeking to enhance their value within a company that is beginning to deploy AI without having to abandon their career path because they fear being replaced by AI.	
AI Fundamentals for Agricultural Sciences	ORGS
AI Fundamentals for Business Analytics	ORGS
AI Fundamentals for Health	ORGS
AI Fundamentals for Natural Resource Management	ORGS

(continued)

Table A.1 Certificate programs by providers (continued)

Title of Credential	Abbrev
AI in Finance	CORN
AI In Healthcare	CORN
AI in Healthcare (Johns Hopkins)	GRT
AI in Hospitality	CORN
AI in Office Administration	UDEMY
AI in the Classroom	NAT
AI Law and Policy	CORN
AI Practitioner	COSC
AI Product Manager Explorer	UDEMY
AI Prompting	LSU
Note: If you are trying to enhance your current career, learning how to create AI prompts is essential.	
AI Skills for Workplace Communications	CORN
AI Skills Fundamentals	WGU
AI-Powered Shopping Ads Certificate	GOOGLE
Alternative Dispute Resolution	UPAC
American Sign Language (Introductory)	ORGS
AML Essentials: Money Laundering, KYC & Compliance	UDEMY
Android Developer (Meta Android Developer)	Coursera
Animal Genetics	UF
Animal Shelter Behavioral Management	UPAC
Animal Shelter Leadership (grad)	UF
Animal Shelter Management	UPAC
Application Software Support Specialist	CIN
Applied Behavior Analysis	SM
Applied Behavior Analysis	PENNS
Applied Computing, Systems and Network	BOISE
Applied Generative AI (Johns Hopkins)	GRT
Applied Machine Learning and AI	CORN
Applied Statistics	CORN
Applied Statistics	PENNS
Applied Statistics in Digital Agriculture (grad certificate)	Illinois
Artificial and Machine Learning (graduate certificate)	GWU
Artificial Intelligence	IndTec
Artificial Intelligence (graduate certificate)	Harvard
Artificial Intelligence & Machine Learning for Digital Agriculture	Illinois
Artificial Intelligence for Business & Innovation (grad)	PENNS

Title of Credential	Abbrev
Artificial Intelligence for Education (graduate certificate)	REG
Artificial Intelligence Foundations	MARY
Artificial Intelligence on Microsoft Azure	Future
Artificial Intelligence: Applied ML, Generative AI & Agents	GRT
Artificial Intelligence: Principles and Techniques	STANF
Arts & Culture Marketing	UD
Arts & Culture Outreach and Advocacy	UD
Arts Management	BISM
Note: One promising area for people in the arts are these credential programs for the management side of the arts. The University of Denver is particularly strong in this area.	
Arts Marketing Graduate Certificate	BOSU
Assistive Technology (graduate)	BOISE
Atlassian Agile Project Management Professional	LINK
Audience Analytics (grad)	UF
Audio Devices & Signal Processing (grad)	PENNS
Augmented & virtual Reality Design	MARY
Autism	REG
Autism (graduate certificate)	TexasT
Automation & Robotics in Digital Agriculture (graduate)	Illinois
Automation Engineer	Coursera
AWS Cloud Practitioner	LSU
AWS Solutions Architect	LSU
B2B Sales Fundamentals	WGU
Basic Audiometry	SB
Battery Management Systems	IndTec
BCS Consultant Advanced International Business	UDEMY
BCS Foundation in Artificial Intelligence Exam	UDEMY
Becoming a Good Leader	STANF
Beekeeping	CORN
Beekeeping	UF
Beer and Wine Studies	BOISE
Beer Essentials	CORN
Note: Beer credential programs offer a way for people to become entrepreneurs in the expanding brewing industry.	
Behavioral Economics Specialist	UDEMY
Biblical Languages (graduate certificate)	REG
Biblical Studies (graduate certificate)	REG

(continued)

Table A.1 Certificate programs by providers (continued)

Title of Credential	Abbrev
Big Data for Policy	CORN
Bioinformatics (grad)	MARY
Bioinformatics (grad certificate)	TexasT
Biostatistics (grad certificate)	TexasT
Biotechnology Engineering	UCLA
Blockchain Essentials	CORN
Bookkeeping	UPAC
Brand Management	CORN
Brand Storytelling	CORN
Brand Strategist	UPAC
Note: Credentials in branding are an excellent way to enhance your position in marketing.	
Budget, Accounting & Financial Management	RUT
Build a Product Platform Strategy to Accelerate Growth	STANF
Building a Diverse Workforce	CORN
Building Energy Efficiency: Technology, Policy & Finance	STANF
Business	REG
Business & Operations Management Excellence	UDEMY
Business Administration	CI
Business Analysis	Fullerton
Business Analysis & Reporting for Accounting (grad certificate)	SNU
Business Analytics	CORN
Business Analytics	IndTec
Business Analytics	Lamar
Business Analytics	SNU
Business Analytics	PHOE
Business Analytics	Illinois
Business Analytics	LSU
Business Analytics (grad)	PENNS
Business Analytics (grad)	MARY
Business Analytics certificate	SJ
Business Analytics Specialization	Coursera
Note: As evidenced by the number of institutions offering credentials in business analytics, it is a hot area. While AI can certainly help in this area, there is still a need for humans to provide human insight as to what the numbers mean and for offering creative solutions to problems that numbers reveal. Note that there more listings under "data analytics."	
Business and Professional Writing	ORGS

Title of Credential	Abbrev
Business Architecture	PENNS
Business Communications	CORN
Business Contracts	CORN
Business Creation	BOISE
Business Data Analytics Prep	UPAC
Business Economics	CORN
Business Ethics	CORN
Business Intelligence	WGU
Business Intelligence Analyst	Coursera
Business Intelligence Analyst (Microsoft Power BI Analyst)	Coursera
Business Law	CORN
Business Leadership	WGU
Business Management	WIT
Business Management Essentials	CORN
Business Management for Engineers (grad certificate)	Illinois
Business Management Foundations (grad)	PENNS
Business Management in STEM	CORN
Business Model Innovation	STANF
Business of Vital Content Creation	ORGS
Business Operations Specialist	UPAC
Business Opportunities & Applications of Generative AI	STANF
Business Process Integration (grad)	PENNS
Business Statistics	CORN
Business Strategy	CORN
Business Sustainability Strategy (grad)	PENNS
Business Writing	CORN
Business Writing	UPAC
Business Writing Professional	LINK
Business-to-Business Marketing (grad)	PENNS
Business Statistics	CORN
Cancer Biology for Everyone	CORN
Cancer Education & Management in Under-presented Communities	Illinois
Cancer Registry Management	COSC
Cannabis Law and Business	RUT
Cannabis Law and Policy	CORN
Cannabis Production and Management	Illinois
Cannabis Law and Policy	CORN

(continued)

Table A.1 Certificate programs by providers (continued)

Title of Credential	Abbrev
Note: The growing legal status of cannabis offers a career path for those interested. For lawyers trying to differentiate themselves, this is also a new growth area. Be sure to look under offerings for hemp as well.	
Career Building in an Online World	LB
Career Coaching	UDEMY
Career Counselor and Life Coach	UPAC
Case Management	IndTec
Catering Professional	UPAC
Note: For those who love to cook and bake, this is an area that can be done part-time to begin and then move to full time when you accumulate enough customers. CE Systems (graduate certificate)	Illinois
Certificated Analytics Professional (CAP) Cert Prep	LINK
Certificated Associate in Project Management (CAPM)	SM
Certificated Chief Technology Officer (52-week program)	UDEMY
Note: This is a long-term commitment (one year), but if you think about it, how does an IT professional gain enough knowledge on the job to become a CTO?	
Certificated Safety and Health Official	DH
CFI Corporate Finance Foundations Professional	LINK
Chakra Balancing with Crystals	UDEMY
Change Management	CORN
Change Management Professional	LINK
Change Management: Reskilling in the Age of Analytics & AI	STANF
Charitable Financial Planning (graduate certificate)	TexasT
Child Development Associate (DCA)	COSC
Christian Ministry	REG
Christian School Administration & Leadership (grad certificate)	REG
Christian Theology (graduate certificate)	REG
Church History (graduate certificate)	REG
Church Leadership (graduate certificate)	REG
Clean Renewable Energy & Storage for a Sustainable Future	STANF
Client-Directed Counseling for Nutrition Professionals	CORN
Clinical Development	SF
Clinical Medical Assistant	CPTC
Cloud Computing	PHOE
Cloud Computing & Networking	MARY

Title of Credential	Abbrev
Cloud Computing & Networking (grad)	MARY
Cloud Security	STANF
Coaching	UDEMY
Coding Bootcamp Certificate	SLO
Coding Bootcamp Certificate	LSU
Note: coding bootcamps are losing their popularity because of AI's growing ability to do simple coding.	
Collections Management for Costume and Textiles	LB
Commercial Real Estate	CORN
Commercial Theater Development Graduate Certificate	BOSU
Communicating with Confidence	STANF
Communication	REG
Communication and Health Management	Illinois
Communication and Health Promotion (graduate certificate)	Illinois
Communications 360	CORN
Community College Leadership (graduate certificate)	Illinois
Community Engaged Learning	CORN
Companion Animal Nutrition (graduate certificate)	Illinois
Companion Animal Welfare and Care	Illinois
Note: There are certificate programs available in both companion animal care as well as in animal shelter management for people who love animals and are looking for a radical career change.	
Compensation and Benefits	CORN
Compensation Best Practices (graduate)	Illinois
Complete AI Automation & Agentic AI Bootcamp	UDEMY
Complete Criminology Masterclass	UDEMY
Complete PGMP Prep Course in Program Management	UDEMY
Complex Decision Making	CORN
Compliance Management	UDEMY
Compliance Systems	CORN
Compliance, Audit & Risk Management	UDEMY
Computed Tomography	BOISE
Computer Forensics Digital and Mobile	Fullerton
Computer Networking	MARY
Computer Programming	SNU
Computer Science	REG
Computer Science (graduate certificate)	Illinois

(continued)

Table A.1 Certificate programs by providers (continued)

Title of Credential	Abbrev
Computer Skills for the Office	LSU
Conference & Wedding Planning (graduate certificate)	TexasT
Conflict Management	BOISE
Conflict Resolution	CORN
Conflict Resolution & Negotiation	RUT
Connect Call Bootcamp	HUBS
Construction Foreman	LSU
Construction Management	EDX
Construction Modeling & Robotics (graduate credential)	Illinois
Construction Planning & Cost Estimating (graduate credential)	Illinois
Construction Project Management	DH
Construction Project Management	Lamar
Construction Safety & Productivity (graduate certificate)	Illinois
Construction Superintendent	LSU
Note: The many construction credentials including project management offer a path for advancement for people who now are doing basic construction work and want to move up the ladder. The University of Illinois ha a particularly strong list of credential construction classes.	
Consumer Analytics Fundamentals	ORGS
Consumer Behavior	CORN
Contact Center AI (CCAI) Platform	EDX
Content Hub Software Certificate	HUBS
Content Marketing	HUBS
Content Writing	CORN
Content-Led SEO with Brian Dean	CLASS
Contract Management	UCLA
Corporate Communications	CORN
Corporate Event Planner	UPAC
Corporate Governance	CORN
Corporate Innovation & Entrepreneurship (grad)	PENNS
Corporate Media	ARKS
Corporate Recruiting Professional	LINK
Corporate Sustainability	CORN
Counseling	REG
Counselling Skills	UDEMY
Counter-terrorism (grad)	PENNS

Title of Credential	Abbrev
CPA Pathways (graduate certificate)	Illinois
Craft Brewing	CORN
Note: A craft brewing credential should be considered as part of the beer credential courses listed earlier.	
Creative Writing	CORN
Creative Writing for Nonfiction	CORN
Creativity and Innovation	LSU
Crime and Intelligence Analysis	Fullerton
Crime Scene Investigation	MARY
Crime Scene Technician	PURD
Criminal Justice	REG
Criminal Justice Administration & Procedure (grad)	PENNS
Criminological Theory and Research (grad)	PENNS
Cripistemology and the Arts (grad certificate)	Illinois
Critical Thinking	CORN
CRM Customization Bootcamp for Developers	HUBS
Crop Protection (graduate certificate)	TexasT
Crop Sciences (graduate certificate)	Illinois
Cryptography and Cryptanalysis	BOISE
Cryptography I	STANF
Cryptology Security Analyst (graduate)	BOISE
Curriculum & Instruction: Bilingual/Bi-Cultural (grad certificate)	Illinois
Curriculum & Instruction: Digital Learning (grad certificate)	Illinois
Customer Service	UPAC
Customer Service Excellence	RUT
Customer Support Specialist (Google IT & Microsoft IT courses)	Coursera
Cyber & Network Defense	PHOE
Cyber Bootcamp	LSU
Cyber for All	BOISE
Cyber Operations	BOISE
Cyber Operations (grad)	MARY
Cyber Practitioner Preparation	REG
Cyber Security (Google Cybersecurity)	Coursera
Cyber Threat Analytics & Prevention (grad)	PENNS
Cyber Threat Hunting	MARY
Cyber-GIS and Geospatial Data Science (grad certificate)	Illinois
Cybersecurity	DH

(continued)

Table A.1 Certificate programs by providers (continued)

Title of Credential	Abbrev
Cybersecurity	LB
Cybersecurity	SLO
Cybersecurity	GWU
Cybersecurity	IndTec
Cybersecurity	REG
Cybersecurity and AI Strategy	CORN
Cybersecurity and Executive Strategy	STANF
Cybersecurity Management	UD
Cybersecurity Management & Policy (grad)	MARY
Cybersecurity Management, Risk, and Governance	SM
Cybersecurity Policy	REG
Cybersecurity Technology (grad)	MARY
Cybersecurity: IT & Data Security in the Age of AI	GRT
Note: For those already in IT looking for a smooth career path, forecasts are rosy for those with training in cybersecurity.	
Dairy Nutrition for Udder Success (graduate certificate)	Illinois
Data Analysis	CORN
Data Analysis for All	BOISE
Data Analysis with Python (300 hours)	CLASS
Data Analyst	Coursera
Data Analytics	Lamar
Data Analytics	MARY
Data Analytics	CORN
Data Analytics (grad)	PENNS
Data Analytics (graduate)	Illinois
Data Analytics & Engineering (grad)	PENNS
Data Analytics 360	CORN
Data Analytics Bootcamp	LSU
Data Analytics Essentials	GRT
Data Analytics (grad certificate)	BOSU
Data Analytics in R	CORN
Data Analytics Skills	WGU
Data Engineering	WGU
Data Engineering (IBM)	EDX
Data Engineering for Analytics (grad)	PENNS
Data Engineering Professional	LINK
Data Ethics	CORN

Title of Credential	Abbrev
Data Foundations for Machine Learning in Medicine	STANF
Data Integrations	HUBS
Data Management in SQL	CORN
Data Privacy Strategy	CORN
Data Science	Fullerton
Data Science and Decision Making	CORN
Data Science Essentials	CORN
Data Science for Machine Learning	CORN
Data Science in Digital Agriculture (graduate certificate)	Illinois
Data Science with SQL and Tableau	CORN
Data Scientist	Coursera
Data Security and Privacy	CORN
Data Visualization with Tableau	CORN
Data Warehouse Developer (IBM)	Coursera
Database Design & Administration	UD
Deaf and Hard of Hearing Education (graduate certificate)	TexasT
Deaf-blindness (graduate certificate)	TexasT
Decision Analytics	CORN
Decision Support for Business	MARY
Deep Generative Models	STANF
Deep Learning for Computer Vision	STANF
Deep Reinforcement Learning	STANF
DEI in the Workplace	UPAC
Demand Creation: Launching and Growing Your Product	STANF
Demand Marketing	CORN
Dental Assistant	CPTC
Design for Packaging Value Chain	SLO
Design Thinking	CORN
Designing and Building AI Solutions	CORN
Destination Wedding Planner	UPAC
Developmental Literacy (grad certificate)	TexasT
Device Design	CORN
DevOps Engineering Foundations	LSU
DevOps Professional	LINK
Dialysis Assistant	CPTC
Didactic Program in Dietetics (grad)	Lamar

(continued)

Table A.1 Certificate programs by providers (continued)

Title of Credential	Abbrev
Digital Advertising	HUBS
Note: Digital advertising and digital marketing are career areas that offer lots of growth opportunities.	
Digital Agriculture (grad certificate)	Illinois
Digital Business Operations	CORN
Digital Design	MARY
Digital Design Suite for Architects & Interior Designers	UCLA
Digital Forensics & Cyber Investigation (grad)	MARY
Digital Health	UD
Digital Health Leader (grad)	MARY
Digital Leadership	CORN
Digital Marketing	Fullerton
Digital Marketing	SB
Digital Marketing	CORN
Digital Marketing	Coursera
Digital Marketing	MARY
Digital Marketing	UPAC
Digital Marketing (Accenture)	CLASS
Digital Marketing (grad certificate)	Illinois
Digital Marketing 360	CORN
Digital Marketing for SMBs	CLASS
Digital Marketing Fundamentals	ORGS
Digital Marketing Fundamentals	WGU
Digital Marketing Professional	UPAC
Digital Marketing Specialist (Google & IBM courses)	Coursera
Note: The sheer number of courses in digital marketing illustrate a need for this information that these institutions are providing.	
Digital Photography	CORN
Digital Transformation	STANF
Discovery Cal Bootcamp	HUBS
Diversity & Equity in Education (graduate certificate)	Illinois
Diversity Equity & Inclusion: Building a Diverse Workforce	CORN
Diversity, Equity, and Inclusion	CORN
Divinity/Theology (grad certificate)	REG
Driving Product Strategy Through Growth and Change	STANF
Drones & Autonomous Systems	MARY
Note: Lots of data to suggest drones are an area of intense growth.	
Durable Skills for Professional Success	LSU

Title of Credential	Abbrev
Dyslexia & Language Based Learning Disabilities (grad certificate)	SNU
E-Commerce Specialist	UPAC
Early Childhood and Family Policy (grad certificate)	TexasT
Early Childhood Education (grad certificate)	CONC
Early Childhood Education: Curriculum Connections	NAT
Early Intervention (grad certificate)	Illinois
Ecology & Sustainable Tourism Planning & Management	HB
Economics & Policies for a Circular Bio-Economy	EDX
Economics of the Clean Energy Transition	STANF
eDiscovery for Paralegals	UPAC
Educational Diagnostician (grad certificate)	TexasT
Educational Leadership (grad certificate)	REG
EE Systems (grad certificate)	Illinois
Effective Management	Fullerton
EKG Technician	CPTC
eLearning and Online Teaching (grad certificate)	TexasT
eLearning Design (grad certificate)	REG
Electric Cars	EDX
Electric Power Technology	BISM
E-mail Marketing	HUBS
E-mail Marketing Professional	LINK
E-mail Marketing Software	HUBS
Emergency Management	UF
Emerging Markets	CORN
Employee Onboarding	UDEMY
Employee Relations and Investigations	CORN
Employment Law	LB
Employment Law	UPAC
Employment Law	CORN
Employment Law for Leaders	CORN
Energizing Entrepreneurs: Food & Beverage	Illinois
Energy & Sustainability	UD
Energy Storage	STANF
Energy Transition Strategies (grad)	PENNS
Engineering and Architectural AutoCAD	LB
Engineering Geology & Subsurface Investigations (grad)	Illinois
Engineering Leadership	CORN

(continued)

Table A.1 Certificate programs by providers (continued)

Title of Credential	Abbrev
Engineering Leadership & Innovation Management (grad)	PENNS
Engineering Management (grad)	ORGS
Engineering Mechanics	ORGS
Engineering Project Management (grad)	ORGS
Environmental Analytics & Reporting	UD
Enterprise Architecture (grad)	PENNS
Enterprise Information & Security Technology Architecture	PENNS
Enterprise Resource Planning	Lamar
Enterprise Risk Management Graduate Certificate	BOSU
Entertainment Industry Fundamentals	UCLA
Entertainment Law and Business	CORN
Entrepreneurship	CORN
Entrepreneurship	LSU
Entrepreneurship	UPAC
Entrepreneurship Fundamentals	WGU
Entrepreneurship in the Services Industry	TexasT
Entrepreneurship Start-Up and Business Owner Management	UPAC
Entrepreneurship and Strategic Innovation (grad)	Illinois
Environmental and Safety Regulations	BISM
Environmental Geology (grad certificate)	Illinois
Environmental Health & Safety	UD
Environmental Horticulture Management	UF
Environmental Hydrodynamics (grad certificate)	Illinois
Environmental Hydrology (grad certificate)	Illinois
Environmental Management	UD
Environmental Management for Sustainability	EDX
Environmental Policy	UD
Environmental Remediation & Compliance (grad)	Illinois
Environmental Sustainability (grad)	Illinois
Note: The large number of "green" classes point to a field that will continue to grow despite dwindling federal support. Specifically, areas such as the need for clean water will continue to grow.	
Equitable Community Change	CORN
Esports	BOISE
Essential Business Skills for the 21st Century	LB
Essential Quantitative Business Skills	EDX
Essentials of Business (graduate certificate)	TexasT

Title of Credential	Abbrev
Essential Skills in Adobe inDesign 2025 Professional	LINK
Ethics of AI	CLASS
Note: **Forecasts suggest that there will be a great need for people in larger companies that focus on the ethics of AI usage.**	
Event Law	UPAC
Event Management and Design	UPAC
Event Planning	BISM
Note: Keep in mind that credential courses for event planning are listed in various ways alphabetically so "corporate event planning" will be found in a different place from "event planning."	
Excel for Everyone	EDX
Excel VBA Analytics	CORN
Executive Compensation	CORN
Executive Healthcare Leadership	CORN
Executive Leadership	CORN
Executive Women in Leadership	CORN
Exercise Nutrition	HB
Exercise Science	BISM
Note: Personal coaching of all kinds is an area that is likely to grow. That includes nutritionists, life coaches, and exercise coaches. These courses are listed a number of different ways but this is an area where a credential can help convince a skeptical potential client.	
Exploiting and Protecting Web Applications	STANF
Family & Consumer Sciences Education (graduate certificate)	TexasT
Family Business Leadership	CORN
Family Businesses: Entrepreneurship and Leadership	EDX
Fashion Design Management	CORN
Film Editing	UCLA
Finance	REG
Finance Essentials	LSU
Finance for Engineers	CORN
Financial Engineering (grad)	PENNS
Financial Health and Wellness (grad certificate)	TexasT
Financial Institutions and Regulations	CORN
Financial Management	CORN
Financial Management (grad)	Illinois
Financial Success for Nonprofits	CORN
Finite Element Analysis	CORN
FinTech	CORN

(continued)

Table A.1 Certificate programs by providers (continued)

Title of Credential	Abbrev
Note: Cornell is one of the few institutions offering an online credential class in FinTech although there is good growth potential in this area.	
Fire Administration	CIN
Flight Mechanics	CORN
Fluid Dynamics Simulations Using Ansys	CORN
Food and Beverage Management	CORN
Food Processing Unit Operations	CORN
Food Product Development	CORN
Food Regulation, Nutrition Policy, & Personalized Nutrition	Illinois
Note: Cornell offers a wide range of classes for the food industry that can enhance the careers of those already holding jobs in this area.	
Forensic Accounting	SB
Forensic Accounting & Fraud Examination (grad certificate)	SNU
Forensic Accounting and Fraud Examination	Coursera
Forensic Behavioral Health (graduate certificate)	CONC
Forensic Psychology: Criminal Profiling	UDEMY
Forensic Science	IndTec
Foundations for Digital Transformation	STANF
Foundations of Artificial Intelligence (grad)	PENNS
Foundations of Clinical Healthcare	BOISE
Foundations of Data Science	PENNS
Foundations of Information Security	STANF
Foundations of Public Health	BOISE
Foundations of Rural Health	BOISE
Foundations of the Hydrogen Economy	STANF
Note: Keep in mind that courses in alternative energy are scattered in several places in this appendix including under batteries, hybrid energy, electric cars, and sustainable energy.	
Freight Broker/Agent Training	UPAC
Frictionless Sales	HUBS
Front End Developer (Meta Front End & IBM Front End)	Coursera
Front End Web Developer	WGU
Fundamentals of Cyber Security	COSC
Fundamentals of Human Resources (graduate)	Illinois
Fundamentals of Machine Learning & AI (AWS)	CLASS
Fundamentals of Teaching & Learning (graduate certificate)	TexasT

Title of Credential	Abbrev
Fundraising Management Graduate Certificate	BOSU
Gemini for Google Workplace	EDX
General AI for Productivity	CORN
General Construction Management (grad certificate)	Illinois
General Health Communications (grad)	Illinois
General Management	PHOE
Generative AI & Agents for Software Development	GRT
Generative AI in Education (graduate)	BOISE
Generative AI Professional	LINK
Geo-design	PENNS
Geographic Information Systems	Fullerton
Geographic Information Systems	UD
Geological Sciences	UF
Geomatics	UF
Geospatial Certificate	HB
Geospatial Technology	BISM
German (Advanced)	ORGS
German (Introductory)	ORGS
German Intermediate I	ORGS
German Intermediate II	ORGS
Gerontology	IndTec
Gerontology (grad certificate)	TexasT
Getting Buy-in for Your Ideas	STANF
Getting Started with AWS Services: Fundamentals	SIMP
Gifted & Talented Education for Teachers (grad certificate)	REG
GIS & Geospatial Technology	UCLA
GIS and Mapping Foundations	ORGS
GIS in Public Safety	UD
GIS in the Environment	UD
GIS Tools and Technology	UD
Global Challenges in Business (grad)	Illinois
Global Food Security (grad certificate)	TexasT
Global Health Management (grad)	MARY
Global Health Program Management	UD
Global Logistics	DH
Global Logistics Professional	LB

(continued)

Table A.1 Certificate programs by providers (continued)

Title of Credential	Abbrev
Global Marketing Management Graduate Certificate	BOSU
Google Ads Apps Certificate	GOOGLE
Google Ads Display Certificate (Google)	CLASS
Google Analytics Certificate	GOOGLE
Google Cybersecurity Certificate	Coursera
Google Digital Marketing Certificate	Coursera
Google Workplace Administrator	EDX
Note: Google and IBM credentials carry considerable weight. Government	REG
Graduate Accounting (grad)	PHOE
Graduate Certificate in Human Resources Management	Fullerton
Grape & Wine Science	RUT
Graphic Communication	ARKS
Graphic design	IndTec
Graphic Design Software Essentials	UPAC
Graphic Designer (Adobe Graphic Designer)	Coursera
Graphic Information Systems-GIS (grad)	PENNS
Growth Marketing	CORN
Harnessing the Power of Geophysical Imaging	STANF
Health Care Administration	IndTec
Health Data Informatics & Analytics	UD
Health Data Science	UD
Health Information Fundamentals for Health Professionals	COSC
Health Information Management	COSC
Health Information Management & Data Analytics	MARY
Health Science	IndTec
Health Services	WIT
Healthcare and Eldercare	UPAC
Note: The elderly population is exploding which offers lots of opportunities for workers as well as entrepreneurs.	
Healthcare Change Management	CORN
Healthcare Facilities Planning and Design	CORN
Healthcare Innovation, Design & Entrepreneurship (grad)	Illinois
Healthcare Law	CORN
Healthcare Management	CORN
Healthcare Operations Management	CORN
Healthcare Policy & Regulatory Leadership	UD

Title of Credential	Abbrev
Healthcare Quality & Safety (grad certificate)	SNU
Healthcare Safety Technician	DH
Healthcare Studies	REG
Hemp Cultivation	CORN
Hemp Genetics and Breeding	CORN
Higher Education Administration & Leadership (grad certificate)	TexasT
Hiring the Justice-Impacted	CORN
Holistic Health & Nutrition (Fully Accredited)	UDEMY
Homeland Security	SB
Homeland Security	IndTec
Homeland Security Specialist	LSU
Horticultural Landscape (grad certificate)	TexasT
Horticulture	UCLA
Horticulture	Illinois
Horticulture (grad)	Illinois
Hospitality Accounting	CORN
Hospitality Labor and Employment Law	CORN
Hospitality Leadership	CORN
Hospitality Management	SB
Hospitality Management	CORN
Hospitality Management	CIN
Hospitality Management 360	CORN
Hospitality Strategy	CORN
Hotel Management	UPAC
Hotel Management and Owner Relations	CORN
Hotel Planning and Design	CORN
Hotel Revenue Management	CORN
Note: Cornell offers a number of courses for the hospitality industry that can help employees already in this industry enhance their career opportunities.	
HR Analytics	CORN
HR in Hospitality	CORN
HR People Analytics	MARY
HR Transformation	CORN
HubSpot Advanced Marketing AI Micro-Internship	HUBS
HubSpot CMS for Developers II: Best Practices	HUBS
HubSpot Content Hub for Marketers	HUBS

(continued)

Table A.1 Certificate programs by providers (continued)

Title of Credential	Abbrev
HubSpot Marketing AI Miro-Internship	HUBS
HubSpot Marketing Hub Software	HUBS
HubSpot Reporting	Coursera
HubSpot SAAS Sales Micro-Internship	HUBS
HubSpot Sales Hub Software	HUBS
Human Resource Development (grad)	Illinois
Human Resource Management	IndTec
Human Resource Management	LSU
Human Resource Management	SNU
Human Resource Management	MARY
Human Resource Management (grad)	PHOE
Human Resource Management (grad certificate)	SNU
Human Resource Management (grad)	Illinois
Human Resources	REG
Human Resources	SaintJ
Human Resources	PURD
Human Resources Business Partner	DH
Human Resources Essentials	CORN
Human Resources Leadership	CORN
Human Resources Management	DH
Human Resources Management	Fullerton
Human Resources Management	LB
Human Resources Management	CORN
Human Resources Management	UPAC
Human Resources Management Essentials	RUT
Human Resources Specialist	Coursera
Human Services	WIT
Human-Centered Generative AI	STANF
Hybrid and Electric Vehicles	STANF
Hybrid Work Strategy	CORN
IBM Certificated Cloud Professional Site Reliability Engineer	LINK
IBM Cybersecurity Analyst Professional Certificate	Coursera
IBM Data Science Professional	Coursera
Note: Companies like Google, Microsoft, and IBM offer well-recognized and respected courses with credentials that, depending on your company, might carry more weight than a credential from a small college.	
Immigration Law	CORN

Title of Credential	Abbrev
Inbound	HUBS
Inbound Marketing	HUBS
Inbound Marketing Optimization	HUBS
Inbound Sales	HUBS
Industrial-Organizational Psychology	SaintJ
Information Accessibility Design & Policy (grad)	Illinois
Information Security Manager Exam Preparation	UDEMY
Information Systems	REG
Information Systems Cybersecurity (grad)	PENNS
Information Systems Security	UD
Information Technology	IndTec
Information technology	CIN
Innovation and Design	BOISE
Innovation Strategy	CORN
Innovative Healthcare Leadership	ORGS
Innovative Healthcare Management	ORGS
Instructional System Design (graduate)	Illinois
Insurance	BISM
Insurance & Finance Management	CIN
Infant Toddler Development for Care Providers	Illinois
Integrated Circuit Design	UCLA
Integrated Marketing 360	CORN
Intellectual Law Essentials	CORN
Intelligent and Integrated Energy Systems	EDX
Integrating with HubSpot I	HUBS
International Education (graduate)	Illinois
International Law	CORN
International Relations	REG
International Relations (grad certificate)	REG
International Trade	UPAC
Interpersonal Skills	LSU
Interventional Radiology & Interventional Cardiology	BOISE
Introduction to AI	UDEMY
Introduction to Blockchain (Amazon)	CLASS
Introduction to Cyber Security	Cisco
Introduction to Cyber Security (Cisco)	CLASS
Introduction to Generative AI (GOOGLE)	CLASS

(continued)

Table A.1 Certificate programs by providers (continued)

Title of Credential	Abbrev
Introduction to Large Language Models (GOOGLE)	CLASS
Introduction to SSCP Certificate	LINK
Introduction to the Natural Capital Project Approach	STANF
Invention and IP Management	CORN
Investment Strategies	CORN
iOS Developer	Coursera
IOT for Agriculture (grad certificate)	Illinois
IT Analytics grad)	PENNS
IT Project Management	UD
IT Project Manager	Coursera
Note: Keep in mind that project management courses are listed a variety of ways in this appendix including by level (Introduction to), area of project management (IT project management, Construction project management, etc.), and by credentials designed to meet project management professional certification.	
IT Support for All	BOISE
Italian (Intermediate)	ORGS
Italian (Introductory)	ORGS
Java Developer	WGU
Java Programming	CLASS
K-12 STEM Advocacy Research (grad certificate)	TexasT
Korean (Intermediate)	ORGS
Korean (Introductory)	ORGS
Labor Relations	CORN
Land, Agriculture and Alternative Investing (graduate)	Illinois
Landscape Design	CORN
Landscape Management	RUT
Landscape Pest Management	UF
Large Language Models	CORN
Law & Higher Education	REG
Law & Public Policy (grad certificate)	REG
Leadership	Lamar
Leadership	REG
Leadership & Ethics	MARY
Leadership & Management (grad)	MARY
Leadership Agility	CORN
Leadership and Equity (graduate)	Illinois

Title of Credential	Abbrev
Leadership and Supervision	SaintJ
Leadership Development	Fullerton
Leadership Development	UPAC
Leadership Essentials	CORN
Leadership for Women in Business	LSU
Leadership from Ancient Rome	CORN
Leadership in Construction Management	LSU
Leadership in Energy and Environmental Design (LEED)	UPAC
Leadership of Nonprofit Organizations (grad certificate)	SNU
Leadership Skills for Professional Success	LSU
Leadership Studies	REG
Leading a Culture of Service Excellence	CORN
Leading Innovation	STANF
Leading Remote Teams	CORN
Leading Through Dialogue and Connection	CORN
Lean Six Sigma Black Belt	UPAC
Lean Six Sigma Green	Fullerton
Lean Six Sigma Green Belt	UPAC
Lean Six Sigma Yellow Belt	UPAC
Learning Design & Leadership (grad)	Illinois
Learning Design & Technology (grad)	MARY
Legal Investigation	LB
Legal Investigation	UPAC
Legal Nurse Consultant	LB
Legal Nurse Consultant	UPAC
Legal Research	CORN
Legal Secretary	UPAC
Legal Secretary	HB
Legal Studies	IndTec
Logistics/Supply Chain Analyst	Coursera
Long-Term Administration (grad)	MARY
Machine Learning	CORN
Machine Learning	STANF
Machine Learning	MARY
Machine Learning Engineer	Coursera
Machine Learning Specialization	Coursera

(continued)

Table A.1 Certificate programs by providers (continued)

Title of Credential	Abbrev
Machine Learning with Graphs	STANF
Machine Learning with Python (300 hours)	CLASS
Macroeconomics	EDX
Magnetic Resonance Imaging	BOISE
Mammography	BOISE
Management	IndTec
Management	MASS
Management	SaintJ
Management	MARY
Management	UPAC
Management	BISM
Management 360	CORN
Management Accounting	UDEMY
Management Accounting (grad certificate)	SNU
Management Accounting for Leaders	CORN
Management and Leadership	LSU
Management and Supervision	DH
Management Information Systems	MARY
Management Information Systems	UDEMY
Management Skills for Supervisors	WGU
Managerial Economics & Business Analysis (grad)	Illinois
Managerial Finance	CONC
Managing Change and Resolving Conflict	LSU
Managing Legal Issues in Healthcare	UD
Marine Terminal Operations Professional	LB
Market Research	CORN
Note: One of the rare online market research certificates offered.	
Marketing	IndTec
Marketing	MASS
Marketing	REG
Marketing	PHOE
Marketing	WIT
Marketing (graduate certificate)	SNU
Marketing AI	CORN
Marketing Analytics	CORN
Marketing Analytics (grad)	PENNS

Title of Credential	Abbrev
Marketing Communication	UD
Marketing Design	UPAC
Marketing Strategy	CORN
Master Beekeeping	CORN
Master in Agentic AI (52-week program)	UDEMY
Note: This is quite a commitment but experts forecast that SMBs and large corporations will need people who have this type of expertise.	
Master Wedding and Event Planner	UPAC
Mastering Excel	UPAC
Mastering Project Management	UPAC
Mechatronics	CORN
Media Content Management	BOISE
Media Marketing	CORN
Media Strategy for Policy and PR	CORN
Medical Administrative Assistant	CPTC
Medical Billing	CPTC
Medical Billing and Coding	PURD
Medical Cannabis	CORN
Note: Just a reminder that courses in hemp and CBD (cannabidiol) are scattered throughout this Appendix under different alphabetical listings.	CIN
Medical Coder	
Medical Coding	COSC
Medical Coding	IndTec
Medical Coding	MASS
Medical Coding	NAT
Medical Coding	UDEMY
Medical Device Engineering	UCLA
Medical Insurance Billing	DH
Medical Office Manager	Coursera
Medical Professional Legal Consultant	UPAC
Medical Records	PHOE
Medical Spanish	ORGS
Medicinal Plants	CORN
Meeting and Event Planning	DH
Meeting and Event Planning	LB

(continued)

Table A.1 Certificate programs by providers (continued)

Title of Credential	Abbrev
Mergers & Acquisitions (grad)	Illinois
Microsoft Accelerator Program in Data Science and AI	GRT
Microsoft AI Professional (AI to OpenAI)	GRT
Microsoft Business Analyst	Coursera
Microsoft Office Skills	RUT
Microsoft Office Specialist Associate	UPAC
Microsoft Security Essentials Professional	LINK
Middle East Politics (graduate certificate)	REG
Middle Grades Education (graduate)	Illinois
Minerals and Vitamins	UDEMY
Mindful Inclusion	CORN
Model Development, Deployment & Ethical Considerations	STANF
Multicultural Marketing (grad)	MARY
Music Pedagogy	UDEMY
National Security Studies	REG
Natural Language Processing (grad)	PENNS
Natural Language Processing with Deep Learning	STANF
Natural Language Processing with Python	CORN
Natural Resource Management	UD
Negotiation Professional	LINK
Network Security	CLASS
Network Security	STANF
New Designs in Fundraising	HB
NLP for Finance	CORN
Nonprofit Administration	UPAC
Nonprofit Management	BOISE
Nonprofit Management	LSU
Nonprofit Management	REG
Nonprofit Management	UPAC
Nutrition and Healthy Living	CORN
Nutrition for Metabolic Health	CORN
Nursing Education (Post Grad)	SNU
Nutrition	UDEMY
Nutrition and Foodservice Professional	SB
Nutrition, Health & Wellness Coach Certificate: 3 in 1	UDEMY
Occupational Safety in Supply Chain Management	ORGS

Title of Credential	Abbrev
Office Administration Management	UDEMY
Omni Commerce Leadership	CORN
Online Ministry (grad certificate)	REG
Online Teaching	UPAC
Online Teaching in Higher Education Environment (grad)	Illinois
Operations Analytics	CORN
Operations and Supply Chain Management (grad certificate)	SNU
Operations Management	CORN
Operations Management	Coursera
Operations Management	PHOE
Operations Management	UDEMY
Operations Management Professional (Jack Welch Mgt Inst)	LINK
Organizational Design	CORN
Organizational Leadership	ORGS
Organizational Communication	UD
Packaging Analytics	SLO
Packaging for Logistics & Supply Chains	SLO
Packaging for Marketability	SLO
Packaging Value Chain	SLO
Paralegal	UPAC
Paralegal certificate	LB
Paralegal Studies	LSU
Paralegal Studies	UCLA
Note: Paralegal is an area of moderate growth (mostly replacements for people retiring, although there seems to be a trend of larger companies hiring paralegals to do work formally done by junior lawyers.	
Patient Care Communication (grad)	Illinois
Pavement Science & Engineering (grad certificate)	Illinois
Payroll Specialist (ADP Entry-Level Payroll Specialist)	Coursera
Performance Leadership	CORN
Person-Centered Counselling (certificate program)	UDEMY
Personal Financial Planning: Accelerated Online	UCLA
Personal Injury for Paralegals	UPAC
Personal Wellness Care	UDEMY
Persuasive Communications	CORN
Pharmacy Technician	CPTC
Phlebotomy Technician	CPTC

(continued)

Table A.1 Certificate programs by providers (continued)

Title of Credential	Abbrev
Physician Practice Management	CIN
Python Developer	Coursera
PL-300 Microsoft Power BI Data Analyst Certificate Training	GRT
Plant Ecology and Biodiversity	ORGS
Plumbing Systems Design	UCLA
Policing and Corrections	IndTec
Policy Advocacy	CORN
Post Masters Certificate in Library and Information Science	SJ
Post-Associate: Law & Paralegal Studies	CIN
Power Business Information	UPAC
PR Strategy	CORN
Practical Project Management	RUT
Pre-Health Professions Certificate	SM
Precision Nutrition and AI	CORN
Prelegal Studies	MASS
Presentation Design and Delivery	CORN
Probability Analysis	CORN
Process Engineering Analysis	ORGS
Process Engineering Fundamentals	ORGS
Procore Construction Management Professional	LINK
Procurement and Purchasing	UDEMY
Procurement Strategy	CORN
Product Costing: Understanding the Financials of your Product	STANF
Product Development	CORN
Product Management	STANF
Product Management	IndTec
Product Management	STANF
Product Management 360	CORN
Product Management: Accelerated	STANF
Product Management: Transforming Opportunities into Great Products	STANF
Product Marketing	CORN
Note: Consider combining a credential in product marketing with one in AI. Professional Bookkeeping w/ QuickBooks	UPAC
Professional Criminology (Fully Accredited)	UDEMY
Professional Fiduciary Management for Conservators	Fullerton
Professional Fiduciary Management for Trustees	Fullerton

Title of Credential	Abbrev
Professional Focus + Google Project Management	PURD
Professional Meditation	CORN
Professional Sales	ORGS
Professional Sales	RUT
Professional Speaking Skills (LinkedIn & Toastmasters)	LINK
Professional Translator	UPAC
Program Management Essentials	UDEMY
Program Management Professional (PGMP)	UDEMY
Programming Foundations with Python	CLASS
Project Management	BOISE
Project Management	DH
Project Management	Fullerton
Project Management	COSC
Project Management	CORN
Project Management	GeorgT
Project Management	LSU
Project Management	RUT
Project Management	MARY
Project Management	PHOE
Project Management	WGU
Project Management	GRT
Project Management	PURD
Project Management (grad)	MARY
Project Management (grad certificate)	SNU
Project Management 360	CORN
Project Management Basics	LB
Project Management Essentials with CAPM Prep	UPAC
Project Management for All	BOISE
Project Management for Project Managers	LB
Project Management Foundations	CLASS
Project Management Fundamentals	SF
Project Management Professional (PMP)	SM
Project Management with Concentration in Agile	UCLA
Project Management with Concentration in Lean Six Sigma	UCLA
Project Management: PMP Basics	SIMP
Project Quality Management (grad)	PENNS
Prompt Engineering for Everyone	CLASS

(continued)

Table A.1 Certificate programs by providers (continued)

Title of Credential	Abbrev
Psychology	REG
Psychology of Coaching	UD
Psychology of Emotions	CORN
Psychology of Leadership	CORN
Public Health Essentials	CORN
Public Relations	RUT
Public Relations	UD
Public Relations Specialist	Coursera
Public Sector Leadership	CORN
Public Sector Safety & Health Fundamentals (Construction)	DH
Public Sector Safety & Health Fundamentals (General Industry)	DH
Purchasing	DH
Python for Data Science	CORN
Python Programming	CORN
Quality Assurance (300 hours)	CLASS
Quality Assurance in Service	DH
Quality Auditing	DH
Quality Decision-Making for Engineering Managers (grad)	PENNS
Quality Engineering	DH
Quality Management	DH
Quantitative Finance	CORN
Quantitative Financial Analytics	UCLA
QuickBooks	UPAC
Railroad Engineering (grad certificate)	Illinois
Reading Specialist (post master's)	REG
Real Estate	UCLA
Real Estate Agent (Keller Williams Real Estate Agent)	Coursera
Real Estate Development	CORN
Real Estate Investing and Finance	CORN
Real Estate Investment and Asset Management	CORN
Real Estate Investment Modeling	CORN
Real Estate Law	CORN
Real Estate Law and Valuation (grad)	PENNS
Real Estate Property Management	CORN
Recreation Therapy	EB
Recruiting and Talent Acquisition	CORN
Refinery Safety	DH

Title of Credential	Abbrev
Regulatory and Antitrust Law	CORN
Reliability Engineering	DH
Religious Studies	SaintJ
Reporting and Analytics Bootcamp	HUBS
Resort and Hospitality Management	BOISE
Restaurant Distribution Strategy	CORN
Restaurant Revenue Management	CORN
Retail Management Fundamentals	ORGS
Revenue Cycle Management	CIN
Revenue Management 360	CORN
Revenue Operations	HUBS
Revit Fundamentals	LB
RevOps Bootcamp	HUBS
Risk Analysis	CORN
Sales & Service Data Analysis & Analytics	UDEMY
Sales Enablement	HUBS
Sales Growth	CORN
Sales Management	HUBS
Sales Operation Specialist	Coursera
Scripted & Complied Programming Languages	PHOE
Semiconductor Fabrication	ORGS
Semiconductor Facilities Design & Management	ORGS
Semiconductor Production Process Planning	ORGS
Senior Fire Officer	UF
Senior Living Management	CORN
SEO	HUBS
SEO II	HUBS
Servant Leadership	CORN
Service Hub Software	HUBS
ServiceNow Application Developer	WGU
ServiceNow IT Leadership Professional	LINK
SHRM Human Resources	CI
Six Sigma	CORN
Six Sigma Basics	LB
Six Sigma Bet (graduate certificate)	SNU
Six Sigma Black Belt	DH
Six Sigma Black Belt	UPAC

(continued)

Table A.1 Certificate programs by providers (continued)

Title of Credential	Abbrev
Six Sigma Green Belt	UPAC
Skincare Coach (professional diploma)	UDEMY
Small Business Management	LSU
Small Business Management & Entrepreneurship	RUT
Small Business Management & Entrepreneurship (grad)	PHOE
Social Media Creator	BOISE
Social Media for Business	UPAC
Social Media Manager	UPAC
Social Media Marketing	EB
Social Media Marketing	Coursera
Social Media Marketing (grad certificate)	SNU
Social Media Strategist (Social Media Marketing)	Coursera
Social Media Marketing II	HUBS
Note: All indications are that knowledge of social media can be a door opener for new hires as well as a way to enhance marketing careers.	
Software Design & Programming	UD
Software Engineering (grad certificate)	TexasT
Software Quality Engineering	DH
Soil Management	TexasT
Soil Science & Conservation (grad)	Illinois
Solar Energy (grad)	PENNS
Spanish (Intermediate)	ORGS
Spanish (Introductory)	ORGS
Speech and Language Pathology Assistant	COSC
Speech-Language Pathology Assistant	EB
Spiritual Formation (graduate certificate)	REG
Sport & Fitness Health Professions, Social & Health Sciences	DH
Sports Business	ORGS
Sports Business Management	EDX
Sports Management	IndTec
Sports Marketing	ORGS
Sports Nutrition	Lamar
Note: Sports management of all kinds is a difficult area to break into, but a credential can help since this is a growth area.	
Spreadsheet Modeling	CORN
Startup Funding and Finance	CORN
Statistical Foundations	CORN

Title of Credential	Abbrev
Statistics and Data Science	EDX
Statistics and Data Science (Methods Track)	EDX
Statistics and Data Science (Social Sciences Track)	EDX
STEM (graduate certificate)	REG
Strategic Brand Communication Essentials (grad)	Illinois
Strategic Brand Communication (grad)	Illinois
Strategic Communications (grad)	MARY
Strategic Healthcare Leadership	CORN
Strategic Hospitality Marketing	CORN
Strategic Human Resource Management (grad)	MARY
Strategic Human Resources Leadership	CORN
Strategic Leadership in Healthcare Organizations	UD
Strategic Technology Management (grad)	Illinois
Strategies for Sustainability	STANF
Strength & Conditioning/Fitness Coaching	UD
Studies in Marriage, Couple & Family Counseling (grad certificate)	REG
Studies in School Counseling (grad certificate)	REG
Studies in Trauma Counseling (grad certificate)	REG
Substance Abuse Counseling	CIN
Super Admin Bootcamp	HUBS
Supervisory and Leadership	UPAC
Supply Chain Analytics	CORN
Supply Chain Analytics	ORGS
Supply Chain Fundamentals	WGU
Supply Chain Logistics Management & Procurement	ORGS
Supply Chain Management	DH
Supply Chain Management	IndTec
Supply Chain Management	UD
Supply Chain Management (grad)	PENNS
Supply Chain Management Fundamentals	ORGS
Supply Chain Professional + Freight Broker/Agent Training	UPAC
Supply Chain Sustainability	CLASS
Sustainability	UCLA
Sustainability & Justice in Good & Environmental Systems	Illinois
Sustainability Education (grad)	Illinois
Sustainable Business	CORN
Sustainable Energy Development (grad)	PENNS

(continued)

Table A.1 Certificate programs by providers (continued)

Title of Credential	Abbrev
Sustainable Management	UPAC
Sustainable Preservation	CORN
Systems Design	CORN
Systems Engineering (grad)	MARY
Systems Thinking	CORN
Tax Compliance and Planning (grad certificate)	SNU
Taxation (grad)	Illinois
Teaching English as a Second Language (grad)	Illinois
Technical Writing	UPAC
Technician preparation	DH
Technology Management	UD
Telecommunications Technology	UD
TESOL—Adult Education: Collegiate (grad certificate)	REG
TESOL—K-12: Collegiate (grad certificate)	REG
Text Analysis	CORN
The AI Engineer Course 2026	UDEMY
The Economics of Energy Transition	EDX
The Foundations of Financial Crime Prevention	EDX
The Role of Water and Energy for Circular Economics	STANF
Theatre Practices	REG
Tourism Administration	TexasT
Transforming the Grid	STANF
Trauma, Resilience, and Self-Care Strategies (grad certificate)	CONC
Travel Agent Training	UPAC
Underground Engineering (grad certificate)	Illinois
Understanding LLMs & Basic Prompting Techniques	CLASS
Unmanned Aircraft Systems	UD
Urban Agriculture (grad)	Illinois
Urban Mobility Systems (grad certificate)	Illinois
Urban Pest Management	UF
User Experience and Customer-Centered Design	Fullerton
User Experience Design	CORN
User Experience Strategy	UD
User Experience UI (UX) Designer (Google and IBM courses)	Coursera
Using Cryptography Correctly	STANF
UX Design	BOISE

Title of Credential	Abbrev
Value Chain Management (grad certificate)	Illinois
Vascular Ultrasound	BOISE
Vehicular and Traffic Operations (grad certificate)	Illinois
Veterinary Assisting	UPAC
Veterinary Science (grad)	Illinois
Victim Advocacy	UPAC
Video Game Designer (Epic Games Game Design)	Coursera
Video Game Developer	Coursera
Video Marketing	UPAC
Video Strategy Bootcamp for Loop Marketing	HUBS
Virtual Hybrid Event Planning	UPAC
Visual Impairment	TexasT
Visualization with Tableau	CORN
Water Science & Conservation (grad)	Illinois
Water Systems and Policy (grad certificate)	Illinois
Watershed Management	MARY
Weather and Climate Risk & Data Analytics (grad)	Illinois
Web Design	MARY
Web Design & Development	UD
Web Design and Development	CORN
Wedding Planner	EB
Wedding Planner	UPAC
Weight Loss (Internationally accredited certificate)	UDEMY
Wellness Counseling	CORN
Wetland Science and Conservation (grad)	Illinois
Wind Energy—Managerial Track (grad certificate)	TexasT
Wind Energy—Technical Track (grad certificate)	TexasT
Wine Business	TexasT
Wine Business Management	SS
Wine Industry Finance and Accounting	SS
Winemaking	CORN
Wines of California, the Pacific Northwest and New York	CORN
Wines of France	CORN
Wines of Germany and Austria	CORN
Wines of Italy	CORN
Wines of Spain and Portugal	CORN

(continued)

Table A.1 Certificate programs by providers (continued)

Title of Credential	Abbrev
Wines of the Southern Hemisphere	CORN
Wines of the World	CORN
Note: Cornell has the most comprehensive offerings in the area of wines and the wine industry. Women in Healthcare Leadership	CORN
Women in Leadership	CORN
Workforce Essentials	CORN
Worship & Media (grad certificate)	REG
Writing Secure Code	STANF
Zendesk Customer Service Professional	LINK

Table A.2 Providers by abbreviations

Abbrev	Name of Institution
ARKS	Arkansas State University
BISM	Bismark State
BOISE	Boise State University
CI	California State University, Channel Islands
CIN	University of Cincinnati
Cisco	Cisco Networking Academy
CLASS	classcentral.com
CORN	Cornell University
COSC	Charter Oak State College
Coursera	Coursera
CPTC	Coastal Pines Technical College
DH	California State University, Dominquez Hills
EB	California State University, East Bay
EDX	edx.org
Fullerton	California State Fullerton
Future	Futurelearn.com
GOOGLE	Google.com
GRT	mygreatlearning.com
GWU	George Washington University
Harvard	Harvard University
HB	California State Humboldt
HUBS	Academy.Hubspot.Com

Abbrev	Name of Institution
Illinois	University of Illinois
IndTec	Indiana Tech
Lamar	Lamar University
LB	California State Long Beach
LINK	LinkedIn
LSU	Louisiana State University
MARY	University of Maryland Global Campus
MASS	MassBay Community College
NAT	National University
ORGS	Oregon State University
PENNS	Penn State Online
PHOE	University of Phoenix
PURD	Purdue University Global
REG	Regent University
RUT	Rutgers University
SaintJ	Saint Joseph's University
SB	California State University, San Bernardino
SDSU	San Diego State University
SF	California State San Francisco
SIMP	Simplilearn.com
SJ	California State University, San Jose
SLO	California Polytechnic State University, San Luis Obispo
SM	California State University, San Marcos
SNU	Southern New Hampshire University
SS	Sonoma State University
STANF	Stanford University
TexasT	Texas Tech
UCLA	UCLA Extension
UD	University of Denver
UDEMY	Udemy.com
UF	University of Florida
UPAC	University of Pacific
WGU	Western Governor's University
WIT	Wisconsin Indianhead Technical College

About the Author

Stan Schatt, PhD, is a futurist with a knack for identifying the future impact of innovative technology. He spent two decades in senior management positions with some of the world's leading global technology consulting firms including Forrester Research. Schatt's more than 40 books include college textbooks and technology guides. He holds a PhD from the University of Southern California, an MBA from the American Graduate School of International Management, and an undergraduate degree from Arizona State University.

Index

Printed and bound by CPI Group (UK) Ltd, Croydon, CR0 4YY
15/10/2026
14982827-0004